CONFIGURING PRODUCTION CONTROL WITHIN DYNAMICS AX 2012

BY MURRAY FIFE

ISBN: 149920633X

ISBN-13: 978-1499206333

Preface

What you need for this Blueprint

All the examples shown in this blueprint were done with the Microsoft Dynamics AX 2012 virtual machine image that was downloaded from the Microsoft CustomerSource or PartnerSource site. If you don't have your own installation of Microsoft Dynamics AX 2012, you can also use the images found on the Microsoft Learning Download Center. The following list of software from the virtual image was leveraged within this blueprint:

• Microsoft Dynamics AX 2012

Even though all the preceding software was used during the development and testing of the recipes in this book, they may also work on earlier versions of the software with minor tweaks and adjustments, and should also work on later versions without any changes.

Errata

Although we have taken every care to ensure the accuracy of our content, mistakes do happen. If you find a mistake in one of our books—maybe a mistake in the text or the code—we would be grateful if you would report this to us. By doing so, you can save other readers from frustration and help us improve subsequent versions of this book. If you find any errata, please report them by emailing murray@murrayfife.me.

Piracy

Piracy of copyright material on the Internet is an ongoing problem across all media. If you come across any illegal copies of our works, in any form, on the Internet, please provide us with the location address or website name immediately so that we can pursue a remedy.

Please contact us at murray@murrayfife.me with a link to the suspected pirated material.

We appreciate your help in protecting our authors, and our ability to bring you valuable content.

Questions

You can contact us at murray@murrayfife.me if you are having a problem with any aspect of the book, and we will do our best to address it.

Table Of Contents

INTRODUCTION

The **Production Control** area within Dynamics AX is a great feature to leverage if you are performing any type of manufacturing within your business, and is very powerful and flexible.

It is able to handle almost anything that you want to throw at it, and is able to handle discrete and process based manufacturing requirements, it is able to perform both traditional and Lean based execution methodologies, it has inbuilt shop floor terminals that you can take advantage of, it has scheduling out of the box, and also has comprehensive costing capabilities that you can take advantage of.

But that doesn't mean that it's complicated to set up.

In this book we will start you off on your way by showing you how you can start using the **Production Control** module to create Bills Of Materials, link them with Routes and Resources, and then show you how you can easily configure the shop floor interface, control the production through work instructions, and finally extend out the costing capabilities by creating Costing Sheet template. Once you have this up and running you will have almost all that you need to model all of your production within Dynamics AX.

CONFIGURING PRODUCTION CONTROL

Before we start creating BOM's and Routes and reporting production, there are a few codes and controls that we need to set up.

In this chapter we will show you what you need to configure in order to make the examples in the following chapters work a little better.

Configuring Production Journals

First we need to configure the **Production Journals** that we will be using to post all of the production transactions through.

Configuring Production Journals

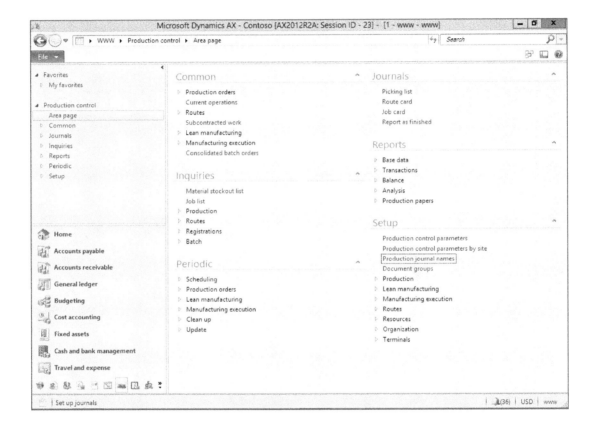

Click on the **Production Journal Names** menu item within the **Setup** group of the **Production Control** area page.

Configuring Production Journals

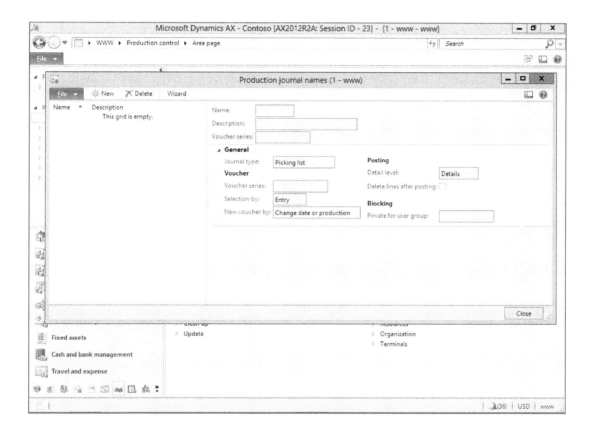

When the **Production Journal Names** maintenance form is displayed, click on the **New** button in the menu bar to create a new record.

Configuring Production Journals

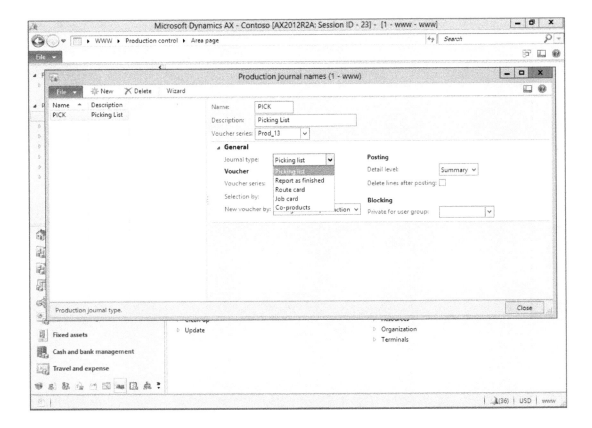

Select the **Picking List** option from the **Journal Type** dropdown in the **General** tab, set the **Name** to **PICK** and the **Description** to **Picking List**.

Configuring Production Journals

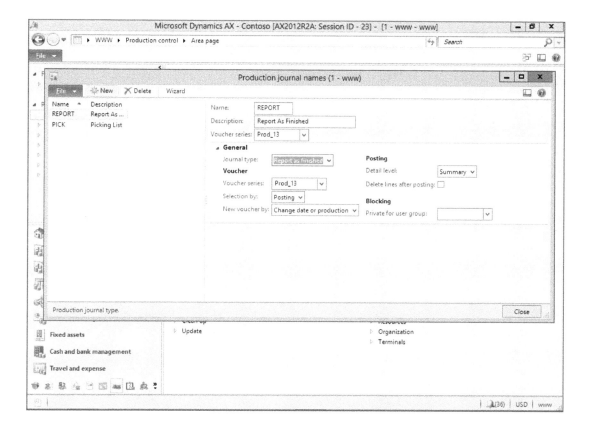

Click on the **New** button in the menu bar again to create a new record.

Select the **Report As Finished** option from the **Journal Type** dropdown in the **General** tab, set the **Name** to **REPORT** and the **Description** to **Report As Finished**.

Configuring Production Journals

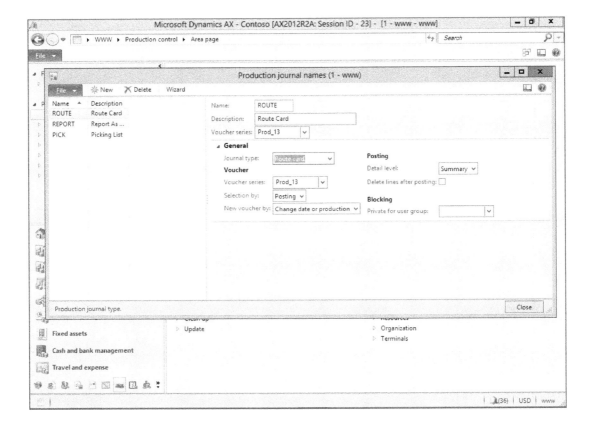

Click on the **New** button in the menu bar again to create a new record.

Select the **Route Card** option from the **Journal Type** dropdown in the **General** tab, set the **Name** to **ROUTE** and the **Description** to **Route Card**.

Configuring Production Journals

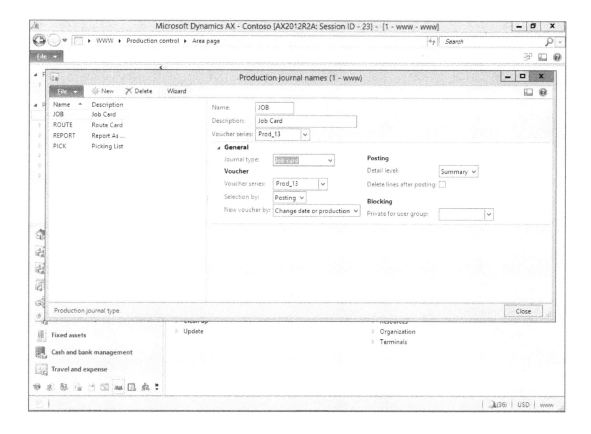

Click on the **New** button in the menu bar again to create a new record.

Select the **Job Card** option from the **Journal Type** dropdown in the **General** tab, set the **Name** to **Job** and the **Description** to **Job Card**.

Configuring Production Journals

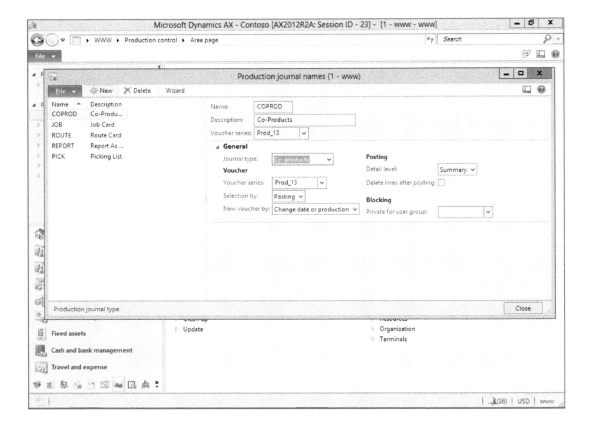

Click on the **New** button in the menu bar one last time to create a new record.

Select the **Co-products** option from the **Journal Type** dropdown in the **General** tab, set the **Name** to **COPROD** and the **Description** to **Co-Products**.

When you are done, just click on the **Close** button to exit from the form.

Configuring The Production Control Parameters

There are also a few parameters that we need to update within the **Production Control** area that will make the production process run a little smoother.

Configuring The Production Control Parameters

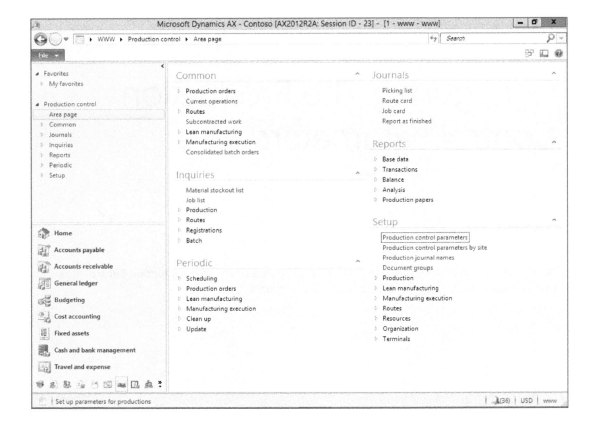

Click on the **Production Control Parameters** menu item within the **Setup** group of the **Production Control** area page.

Configuring The Production Control Parameters

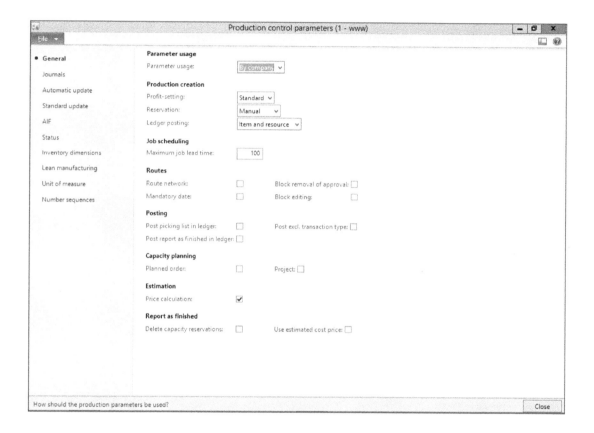

When the **Production Control Parameters** maintenance form is displayed, select the **General** page group (it it's not already selected).

Configuring The Production Control Parameters

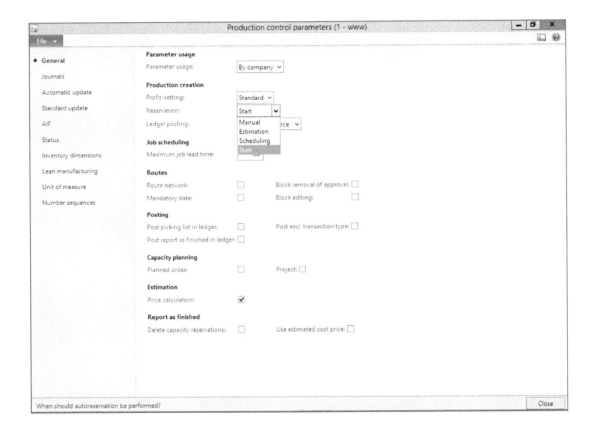

The first tweak to the parameters that we will make is to set the **Reservation** field to **Start**.

This just indicates that the system will reserve the inventory when we start the job rather than when the job is created. That way we won't consume all of our inventory by creating a number of jobs that have not been planned yet.

Configuring The Production Control Parameters

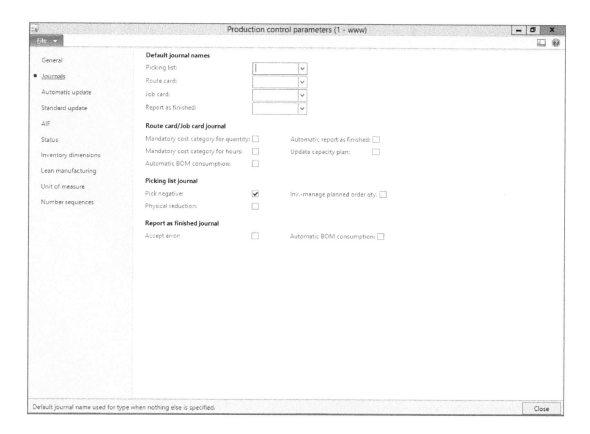

Next, switch to the **Journals** group.

Configuring The Production Control Parameters

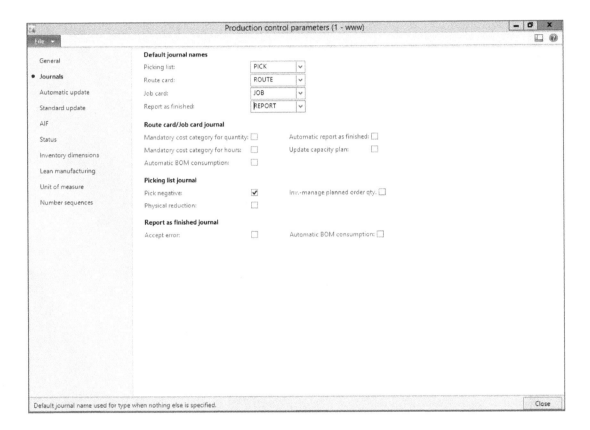

Set the **Default Journal Names** to be the journals that you just created in the previous step.

Configuring The Production Control Parameters

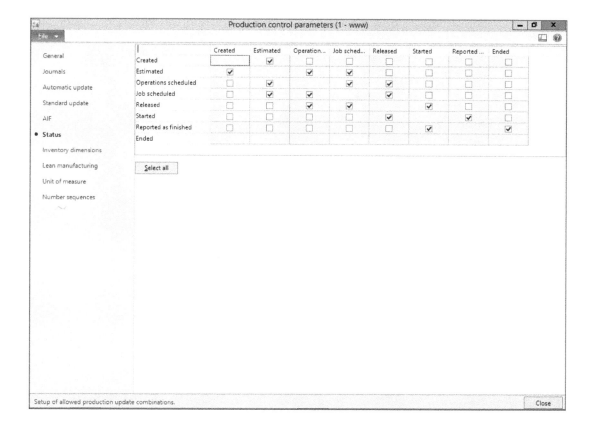

Finally, switch to the **Status** group.

These parameters specify what actions can be performed from which stage in the production process. If you want your production to be very linier where you create the job, then estimate, and then start etc. then you can leave this how it is.

Configuring The Production Control Parameters

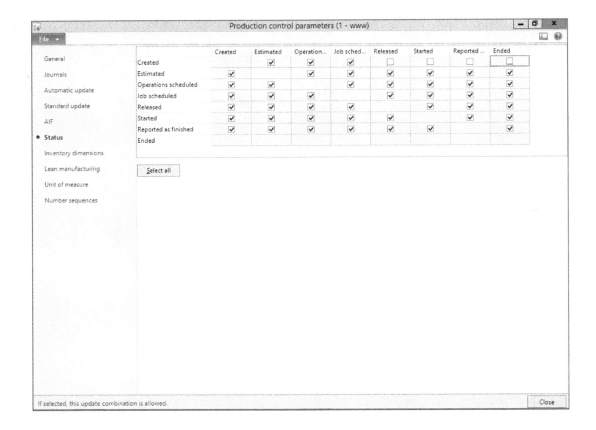

But in the case we will check almost all of the boxes so that we can move our production order to any stage that we like without Dynamics AX complaining too much.

When you have set up your status flow rules, you can click on the **Close** button and exit from the form.

Configuring Working Time Templates

Next we need to configure our production calendars, but before we can do that we need to set up our working time template that we will use to define the hours that our workers will typically work.

Configuring Working Time Templates

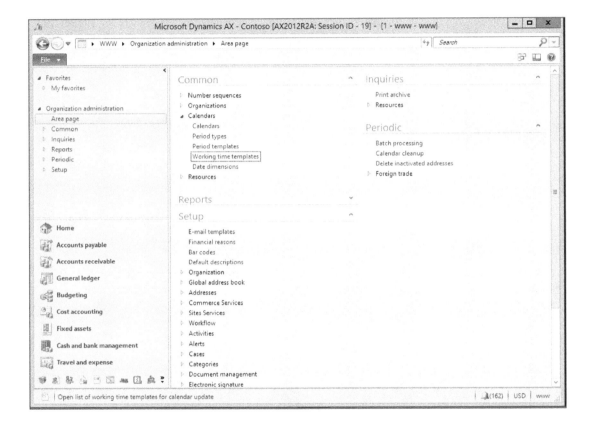

To do this, click on the **Working Time Templates** menu item within the **Calendars** folder of the **Common** group of the **Organization Administration** area page.

Configuring Working Time Templates

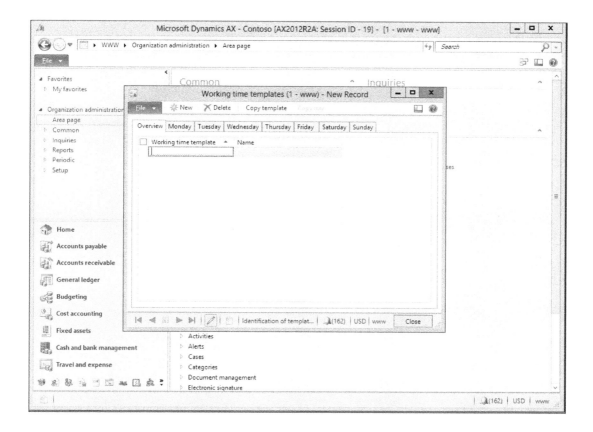

When the **Working Time Templates** maintenance form is displayed, click on the **New** button in the menu bar to create a new record.

Configuring Working Time Templates

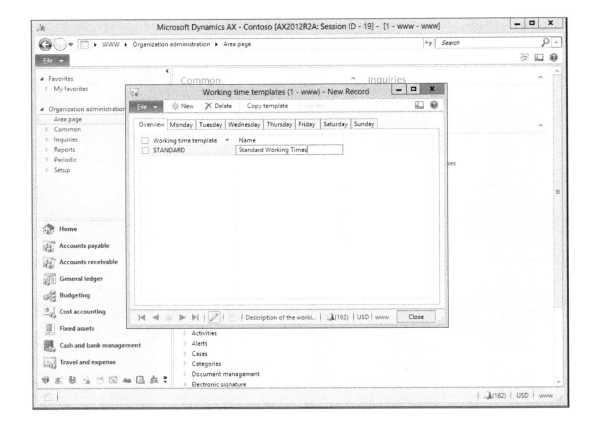

Give your template a **Working Time Template** code and **Name.**

Configuring Working Time Templates

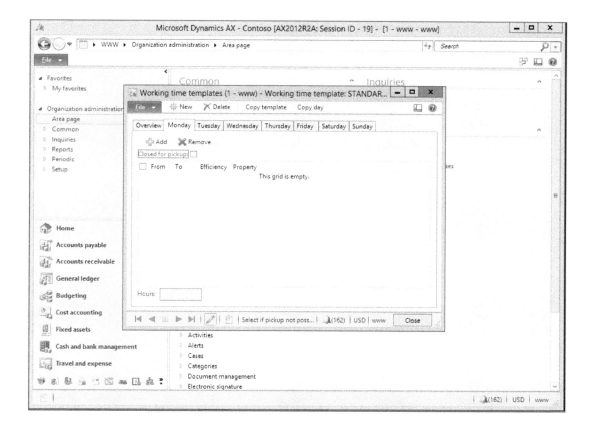

Switch the tab to **Monday** and click on the **Add** button to create a new work shift.

Configuring Working Time Templates

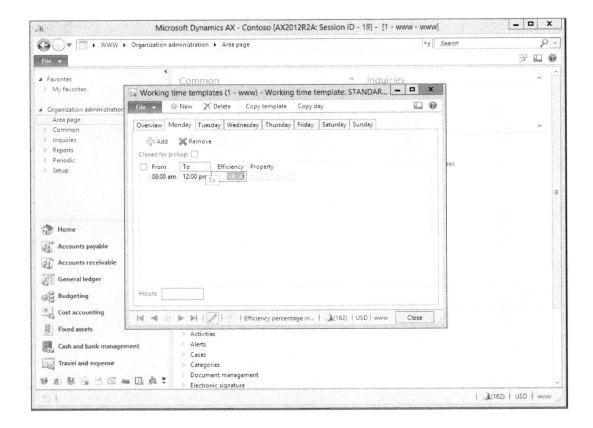

Set the **From**, and **To** times that you want to assign to the shift, and then adjust the **Efficiency** level for the shift.

Configuring Working Time Templates

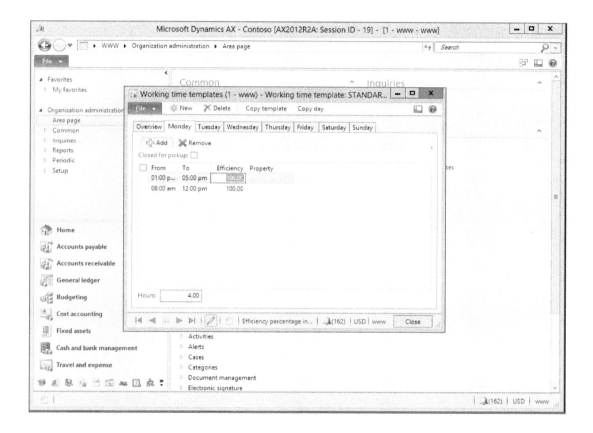

Keep on adding shifts to your **Monday** record until all of the working times have been defined.

Configuring Working Time Templates

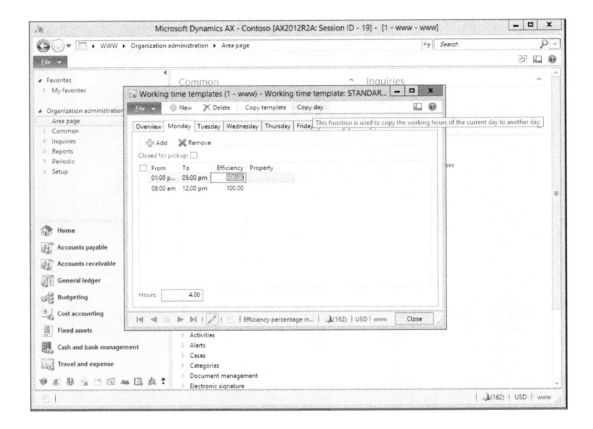

Rather than repeating this for each of the other days in the week, once you have set up the **Monday** times, just click on the **Copy Day** button in the menu bar.

Configuring Working Time Templates

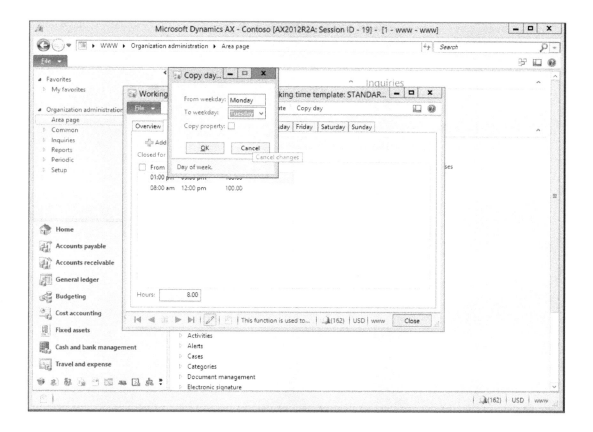

When the **Copy Day** dialog box is displayed, it will allow you to copy the times to any other day record.

Configuring Working Time Templates

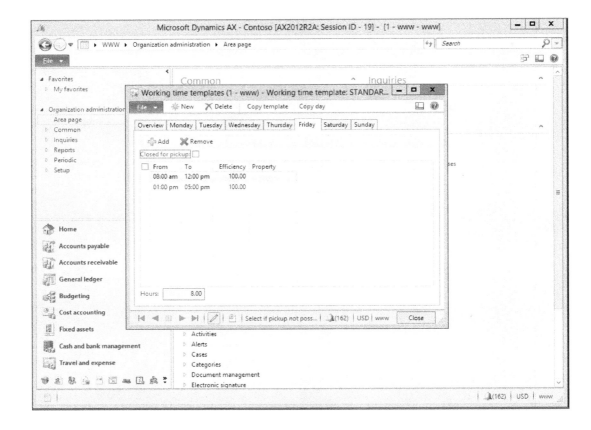

Just repeat the copy process for all of your working days, and when you have finished configuring the working time template, click on the **Close** button to exit from the form.

Configuring Calendars

Now that we have created our working time template, we can use it to create a working **Calendar** that will be used by production for scheduling.

Configuring Calendars

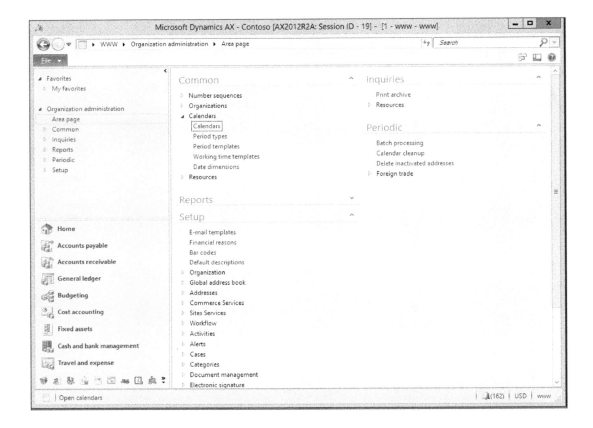

To define a new **Calendar** click on the **Calendars** menu item within the **Calendars** folder of the **Common** group of the **Organization Administration** area page.

Configuring Calendars

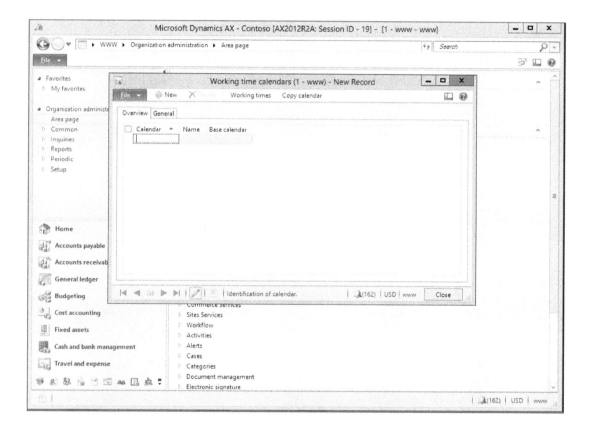

When the **Working Time Calendar** maintenance form is displayed, click on the **New** button in the menu bar to create a new record.

Configuring Calendars

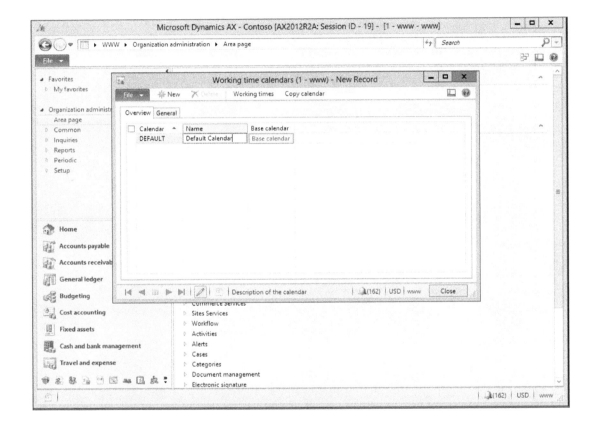

Give your new record a **Calendar** code, and also a **Name**.

Then to populate the calendar from the working template, click on the **Working times** button in the menu bar.

Configuring Calendars

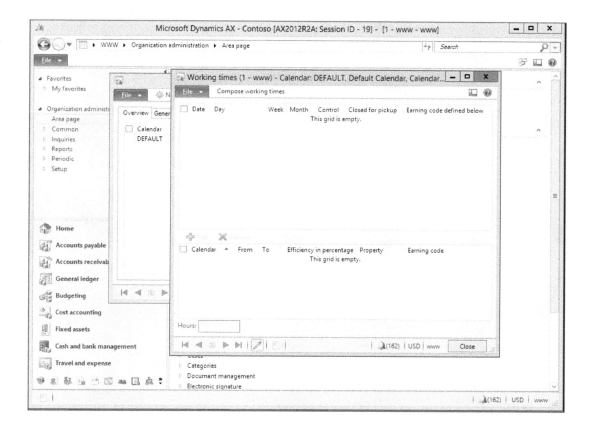

When the **Working Times** maintenance form is displayed, click on the **Compose Working Times** button in the menu bar.

Configuring Calendars

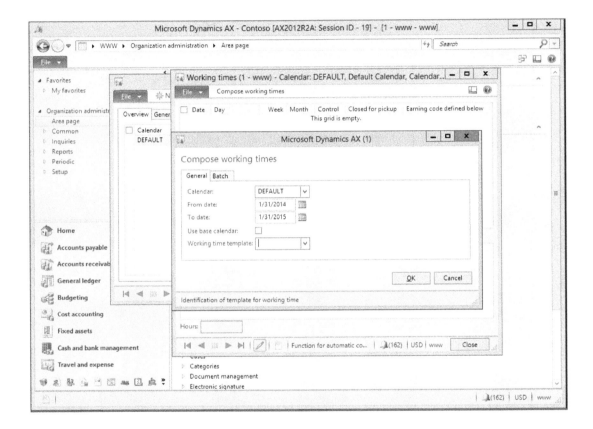

Within the **Compose Working Times** dialog box, select your **From Date** and **To Date** that you want to build your calendar times within.

Configuring Calendars

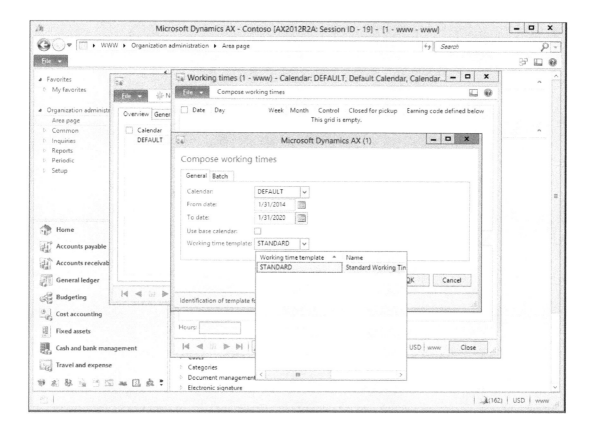

Then select your shift calendar from the **Working Time Template** dropdown. When you are ready to populate your calendar, just click the **OK** button.

Configuring Calendars

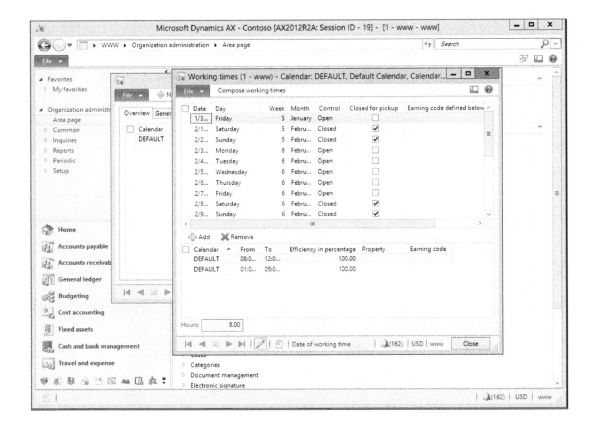

When you return back to your **Working Times** form, you will see that every day is now populated, along with the shift times.

You can now close out of all the forms.

Configuring Production Units

Finally we will finish up the setup by creating a **Production Unit** so that we can link our warehouses and jobs together. The Production Units are used to ensure that common production jobs are kept within the same group of warehouses etc.

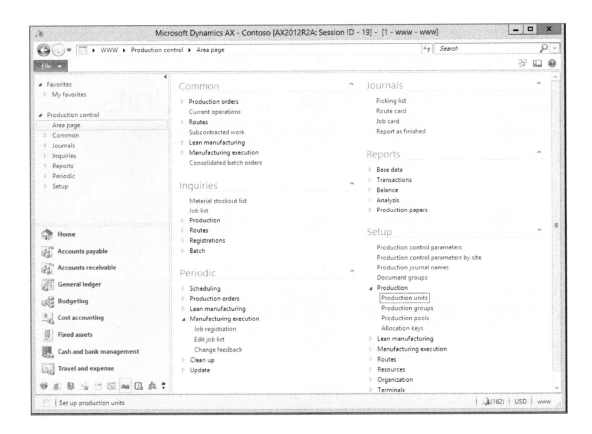

To do this, click on the **Production Units** menu item within the **Production** folder of the **Setup** group within the **Production Control** area page.

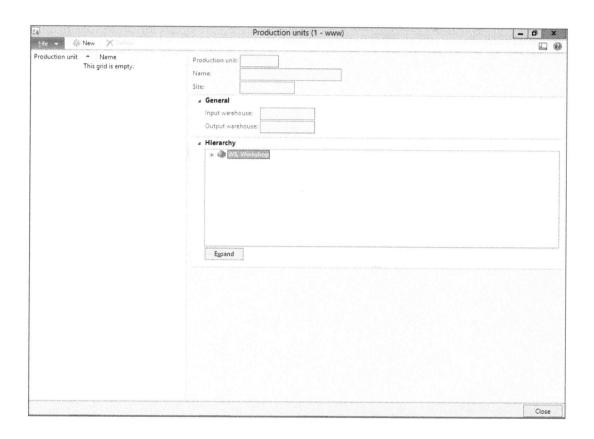

When the **Production Units** maintenance form is displayed, click on the **New** button within the menu bar to create a new record.

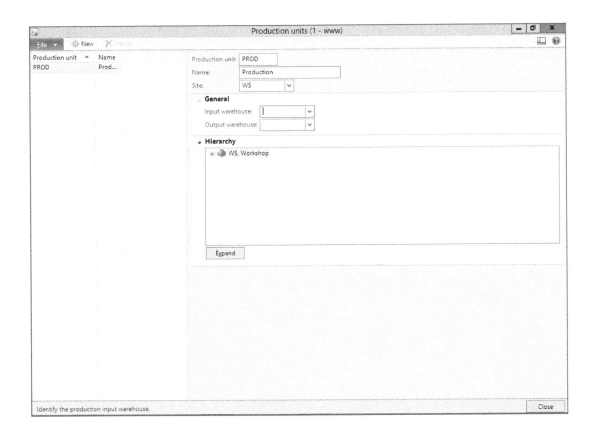

Assign your new record a **Production Unit** code, **Name**, and link it with your production units main site.

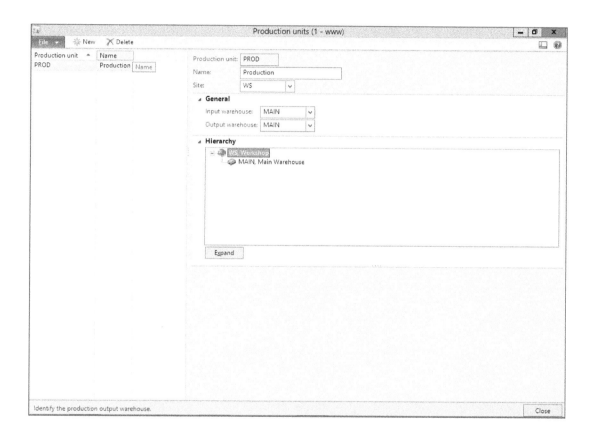

Within the **General** tab, you can also specify the primary **Input Warehouse** and **Output Warehouse** to help with the defaulting of the location details.

When you have finished setting up the **Production Unit** just click the **Close** button to exit from the form.

CONFIGURING BILLS OF MATERIALS

The first step in the process of configuring Production is to mark your products as having a Bill Of Material behind it, and then creating for Bill Of Materials for the product. Once you have done that, you have all of the structure in place to perform cost roll ups and calculate the material costs of the product.

In this chapter we will walk you through the steps that you need to work through to do just that.

Marking a Product As BOM Based Product

Before we can create a Bill Of Materials for a product, we need to mark it as a Bill Of Materials Based product.

In this section we will show how to mark a product as a BOM based product.

Marking a Product As BOM Based Product

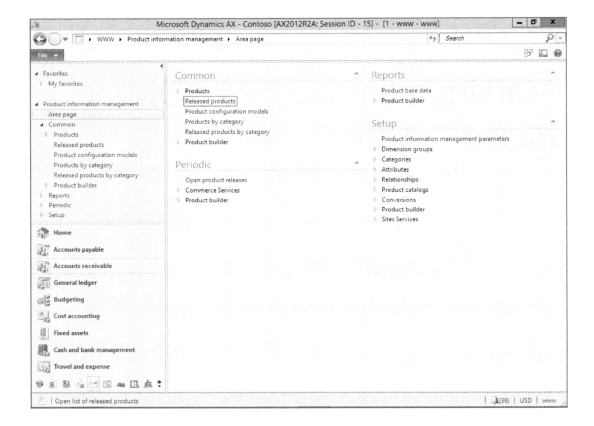

Click on the **Released Products** menu item within the **Common** group of the **Product Information Management** area page.

Marking a Product As BOM Based Product

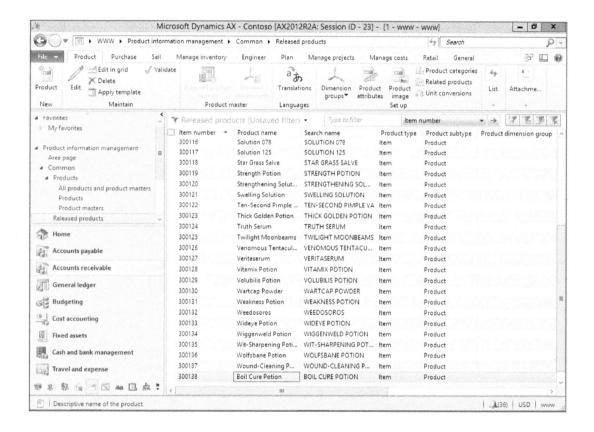

When the **Release Products** list page is displayed, select the product that you want to configure with a **BOM.**

Marking a Product As BOM Based Product

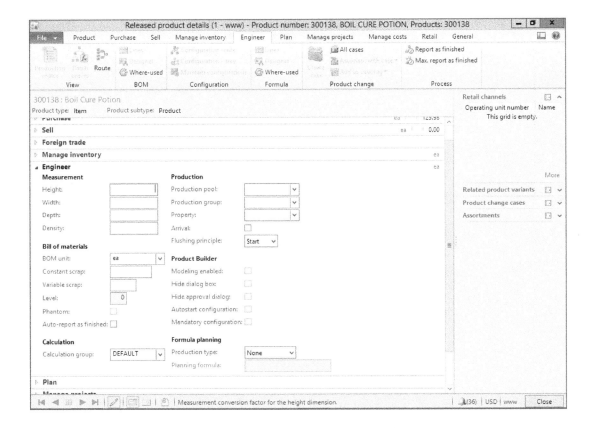

When the **Released Product Details** page is displayed, scroll down until you get to the **Engineer** group tab, and expand it.

Marking a Product As BOM Based Product

Select the **Production Type** field within the **Formula Planning** group, and change the value to **BOM.**

Marking a Product As BOM Based Product

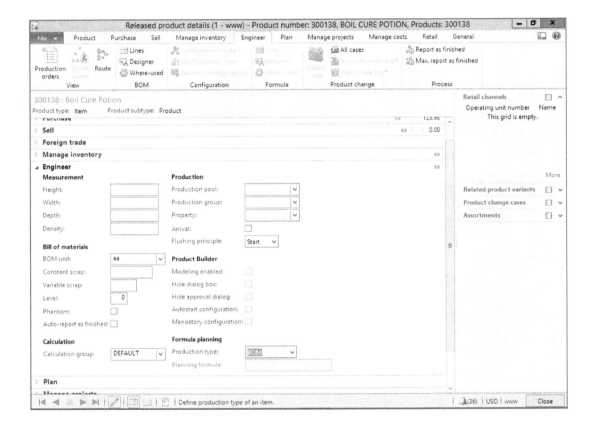

When you have finished, you can click the **Close** button to exit out of the form and save the changes.

Creating a Bill Of Materials For A Product

Once a product is marked as a BOM based product, you can then build a Bill of Materials for it from within the Engineering ribbon bar.

In this section we will show you how you can build a new BOM for your product.

Creating a Bill Of Materials For A Product

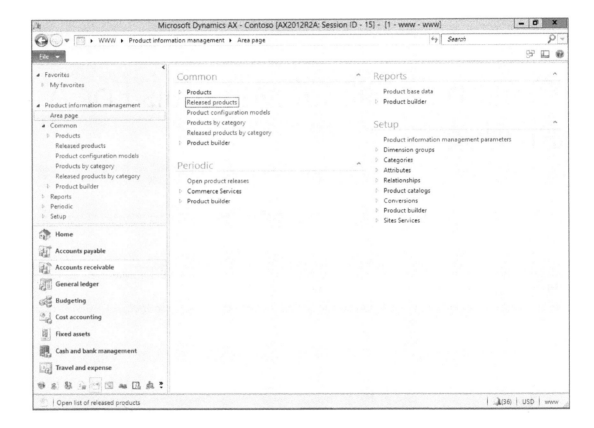

Click on the **Released Products** menu item within the **Common** group of the **Product Information Management** area page.

Creating a Bill Of Materials For A Product

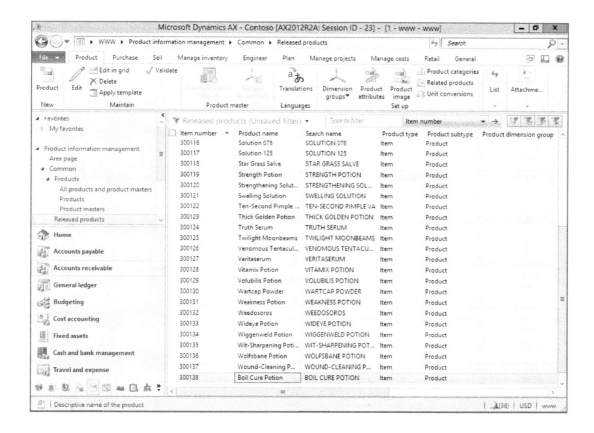

When the **Release Products** list page is displayed, select the product that you want to configure with a **BOM.**

Creating a Bill Of Materials For A Product

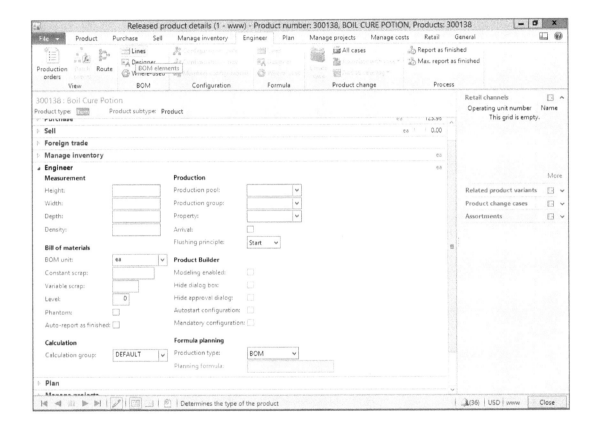

Click on the **Lines** menu button from within the **BOM** group of the **Engineer** ribbon bar.

Creating a Bill Of Materials For A Product

When the **BOM Line** maintenance form is displayed, click on the **Create BOM** button within the **Versions** menu bar.

Creating a Bill Of Materials For A Product

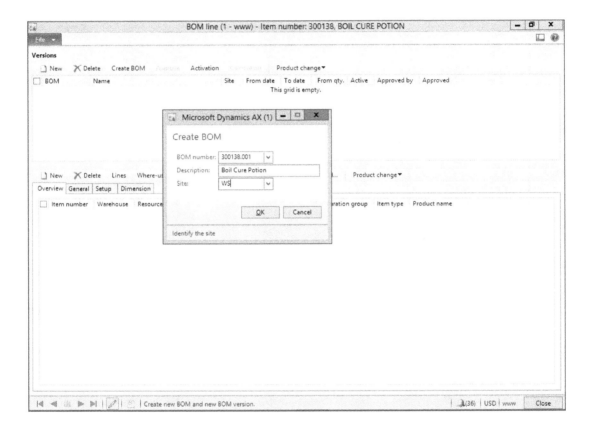

This will open up a **Create BOM** dialog box. Give your BOM a **BOM Number**, a **Description** and also assign it to a **Site**.

When you have done that click on the **OK** button to create your BOM.

Creating a Bill Of Materials For A Product

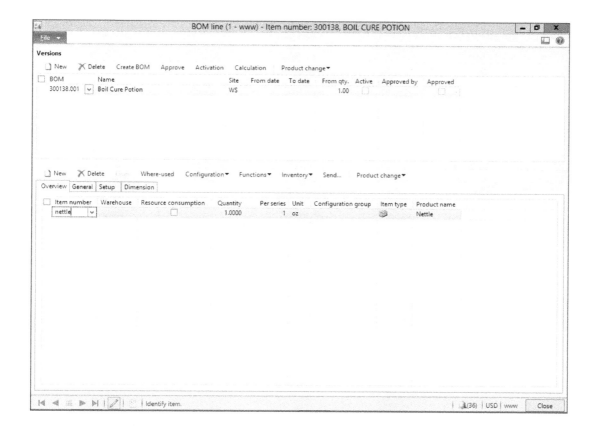

Now you can click on the **New** button within the **BOM Lines** menu bar to start adding your BOM Lines.

Enter in the **Item Number** for the first item in the BOM and also specify a **Quantity**.

Creating a Bill Of Materials For A Product

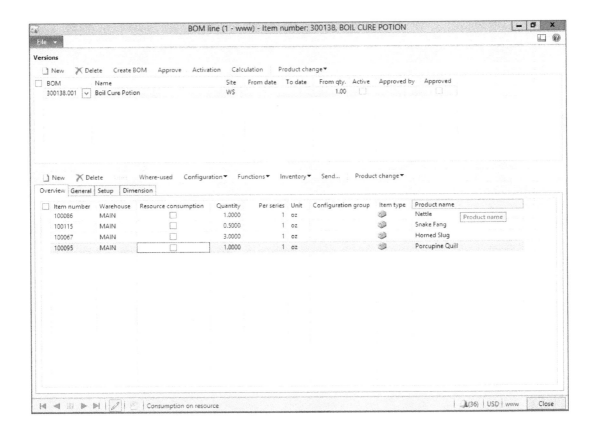

Repeat the process for all of the items that you have in your BOM.

Once you are done, you can click the **Close** button to exit the form.

Approving Your BOM

Once you have designed your products BOM, you need to approve it for use. This allows you to use the BOM in any production order.

In this section we will show how you can approve your BOM.

Approving Your BOM

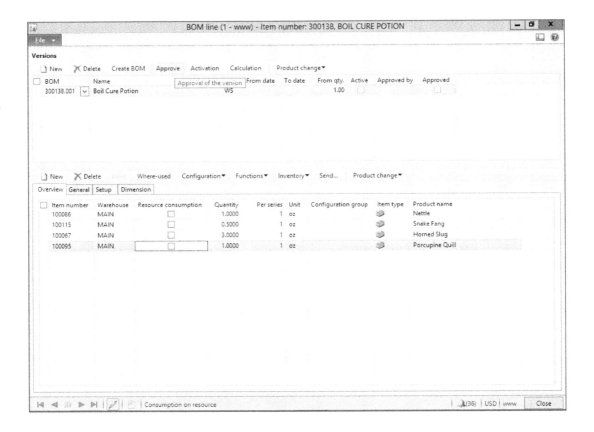

Return to your products BOM editor, and select the BOM that you want to approve.

Then click on the **Approve** button within the **Versions** menu bar.

Approving Your BOM

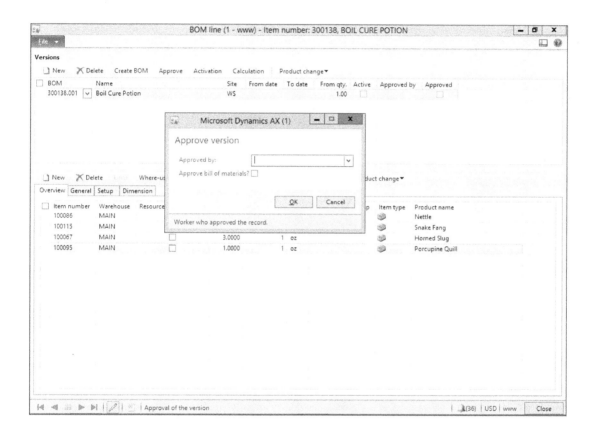

This will open up the **Approve BOM** dialog box.

Approving Your BOM

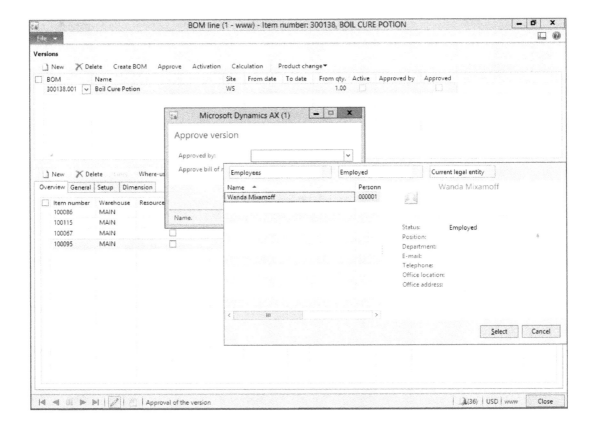

Click on the **Approved by** dropdown box, select your username from the list of users, and then click on the **Select** button.

Approving Your BOM

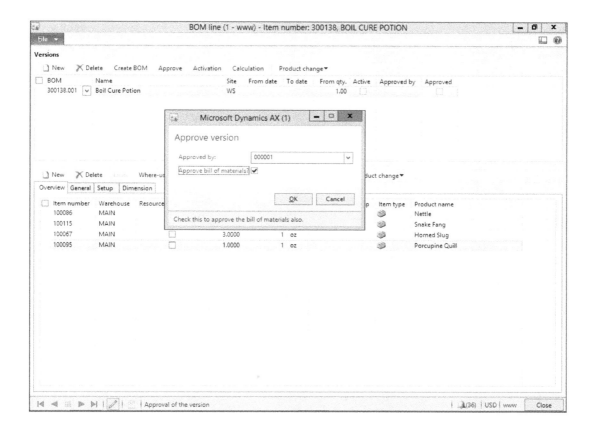

Check the **Approve bill of materials** check box to mark the BOM as approved, and then click on the **OK** button to approve the BOM.

Approving Your BOM

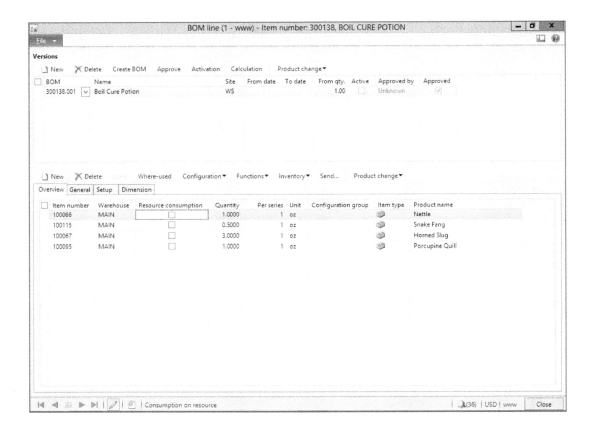

When you return to the BOM Lines, the **Approved** flag should be checked.

Activating Your Default BOM

Once you have approved your BOM, you can then activate it. This will make the BOM the default whenever future production orders are created. There can also only be one BOM activated for your product at any one time.

In this section we will show how you can activate your BOM.

Activating Your Default BOM

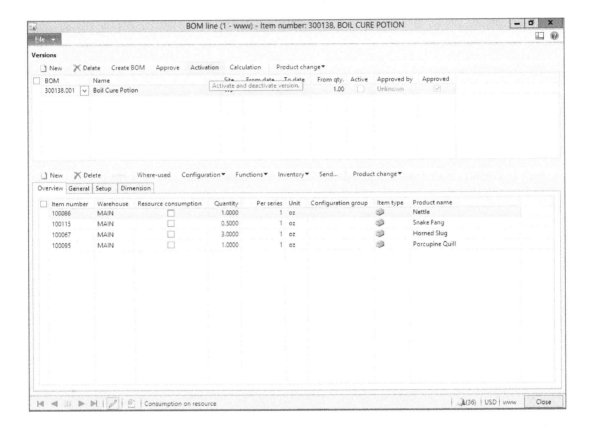

Return to your products BOM editor, and select the BOM that you want to approve.

Then click on the **Activation** button within the **Versions** menu bar.

Activating Your Default BOM

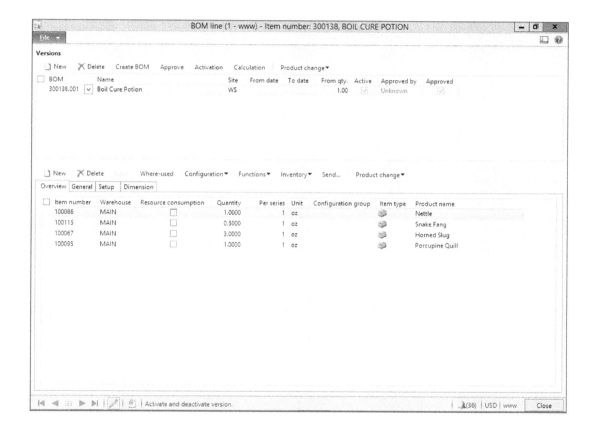

Now when you look at the BOM Lines, the **Active** flag should be checked.

Viewing the BOM in the Designer Mode

The BOM editor has an additional feature that allows you to view the BOM as an indented tree structure as well. This makes it easier to see all of the components of the BOM, and also any subcomponents as well if you have a more complex structure.

In this section we will show how you can access the **Designer** mode to view your BOM's.

Viewing the BOM in the Designer Mode

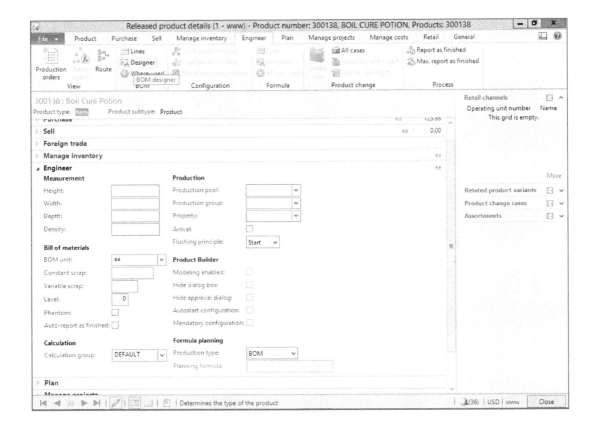

Open up the **Released Product** that you want to view the BOM for, and click on the **Designer** button within the **BOM** group of the **Engineer** ribbon bar.

Viewing the BOM in the Designer Mode

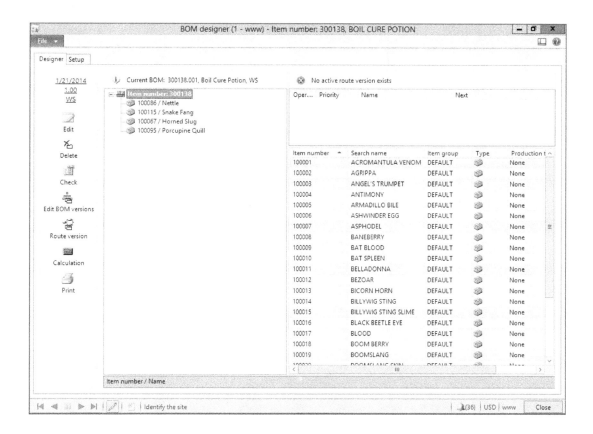

When the **BOM Designer** is displayed, you will be able to see all of the items in the BOM, and also if you want you can add lines to the BOM just by dragging and dropping the components fro the right hand side of the BOM Designer onto the BOM canvas.

Viewing the BOM in the Designer Mode

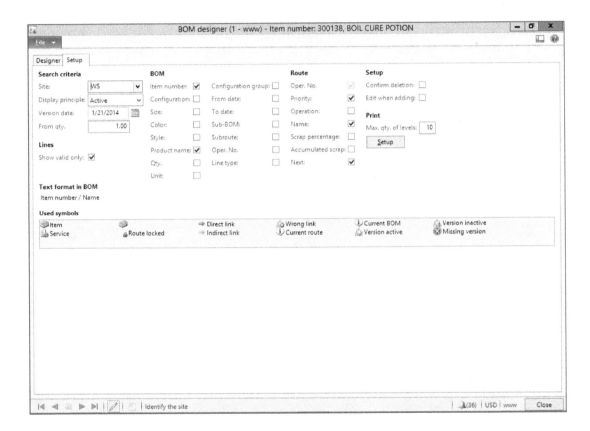

If the BOM is not showing correctly, then switch to the **Setup** tab on the **BOM Designer** and check that the **Site** has been populated.

As a side note, this section allows you to pick and choose the different information that shows up within the lines of the designer.

Blocking Users From Editing BOMs Once Activated

If you want to control the versions of your BOM more stringently and not allow users to make changes to them once they have been activated then you can enable this through the Inventory and Warehouse Management parameters.

In this section we will show how you can block changes to BOM's once they have been approved.

Blocking Users From Editing BOMs Once Activated

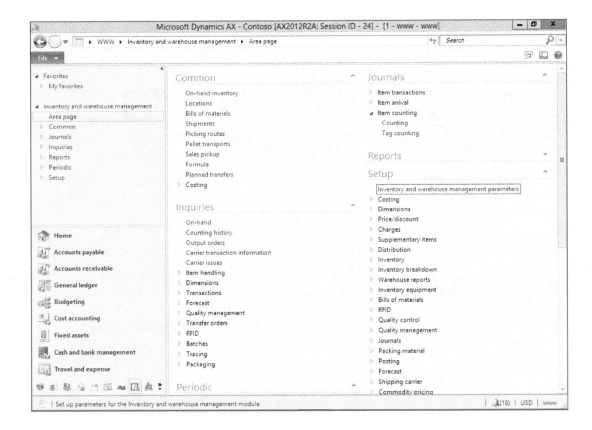

Click on the **Inventory and Warehouse management parameters** menu item within the **Setup** group of the **Inventory and Warehouse Management** area page.

Blocking Users From Editing BOMs Once Activated

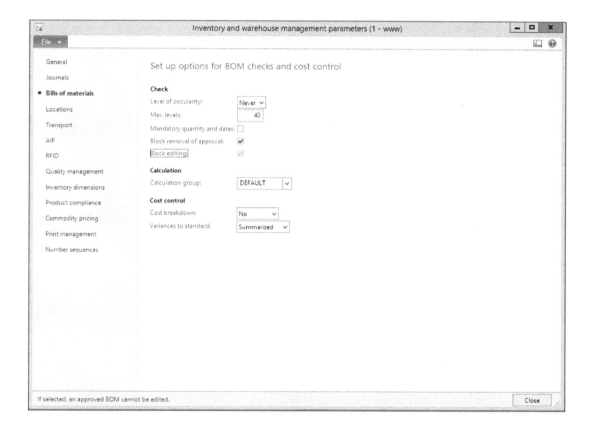

When the **Inventory and Warehouse Management Parameters** maintenance form is displayed, select the **Bills of Material** tab.

If you want to stop the BOM's from being unapproved after approval, then just click on the **Block removal of approval** checkbox.

If you want to stop the users from modifying approved BOM's then you can also check the **Block Editing** checkbox.

When you have made the updates, just click the **Close** button to exit the form.

Printing the BOM Within the Designer Mode

The **BOM Designer** has a couple of additional features built into it that you may want to take advantage of, and one of them is the ability to print out a copy of the BOM.

In this section we will show how you can print the BOM structure from the **BOM Designer**.

Printing the BOM Within the Designer Mode

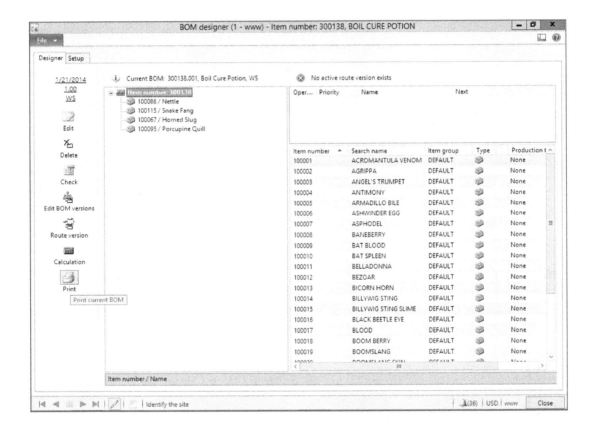

From within the **BOM Designer**, click on the **Print** button on the left hand side of the **Designer** tab.

Printing the BOM Within the Designer Mode

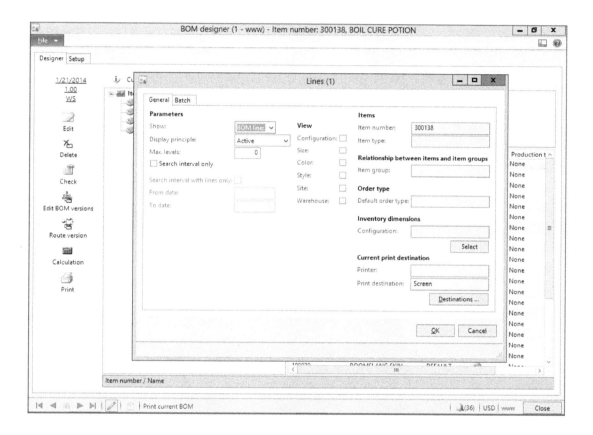

When the print parameters are displayed, just click on the **OK** button to accept the defaults.

Printing the BOM Within the Designer Mode

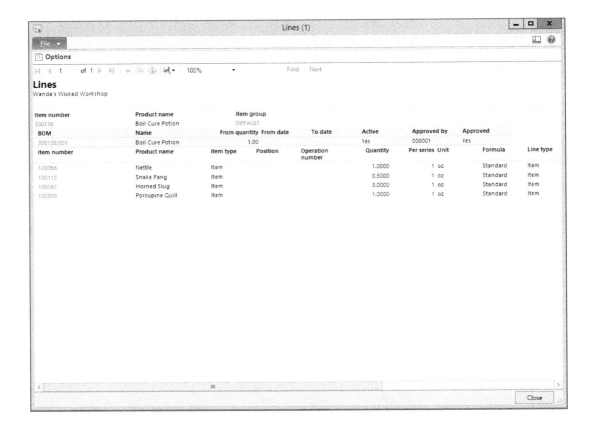

This will create a report for you with all the BOM Details.

Setting Product Production Site Defaults

In order to streamline your production processes for your products, it is a good idea to set the default site settings against your products to reflect this. By making these tweaks, Dynamics AX will know to use production orders when the product is required, and also know where to product the product by default.

In this section we will show how to configure your Released Product to be production ready.

Setting Product Production Site Defaults

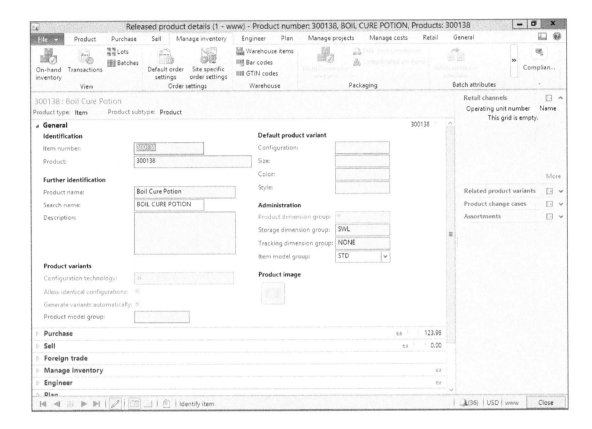

Open up your released product and click on the **Default Order Settings** button within the **Order Settings** group of the **Manage Inventory** ribbon bar.

Setting Product Production Site Defaults

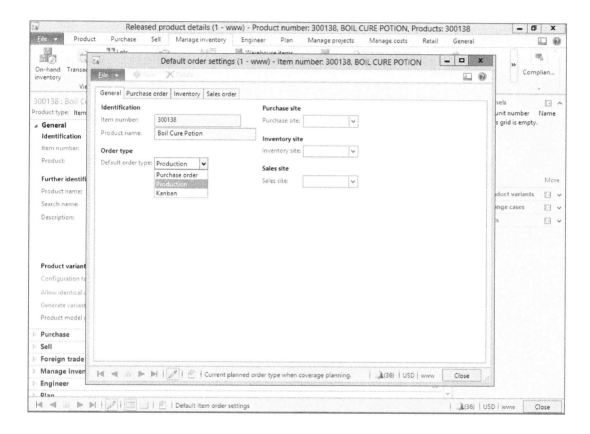

When the **Default Order Settings** maintenance form is displayed, change the **Default Order Type** field to **Production** to identify that the product is to be sourced through production orders rather than the default of purchase orders.

Setting Product Production Site Defaults

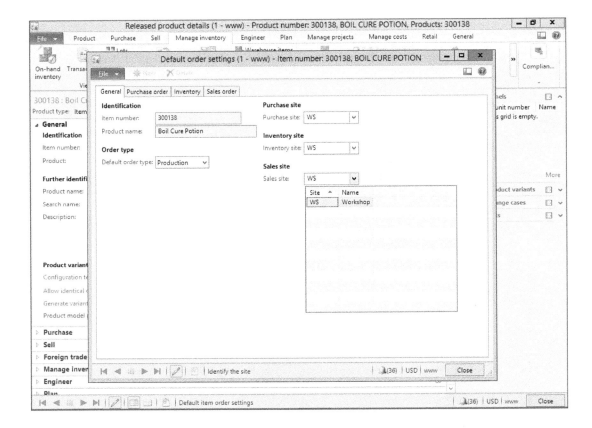

While you are in this form, you may also want to set the default sites for **Purchasing**, **Inventory**, and **Sales**.

Setting Product Production Site Defaults

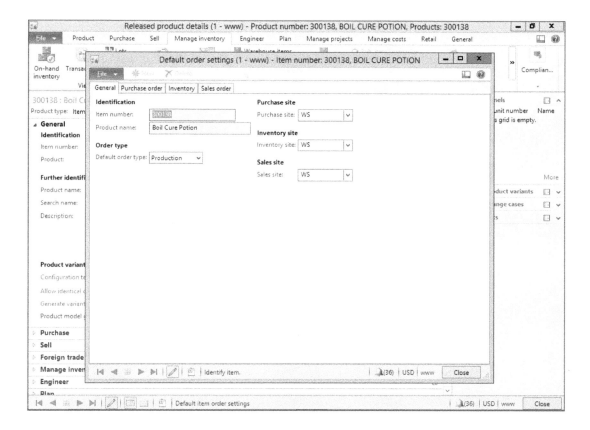

When you are finished, just click on the **Close** button to exit the form.

Performing a Manual Cost Roll Up

Once you have your BOM configured, you can run an initial **Cost Rollup** against it to find out how much it is going to cost to produce. Since we don't have any routes associated with our BOM yet, this will be a pure material cost, but it's a start.

In this section we will show how to run a **Cost Rollup** against a product.

Performing a Manual Cost Roll Up

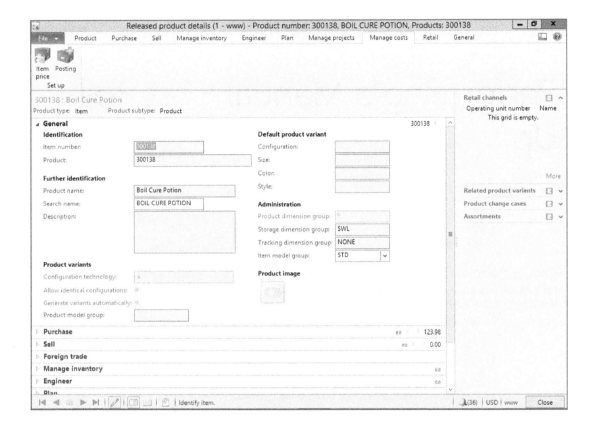

Open up your released product and click on the **Item Price** button within the **Set up** group of the **Manage Costs** ribbon bar.

Performing a Manual Cost Roll Up

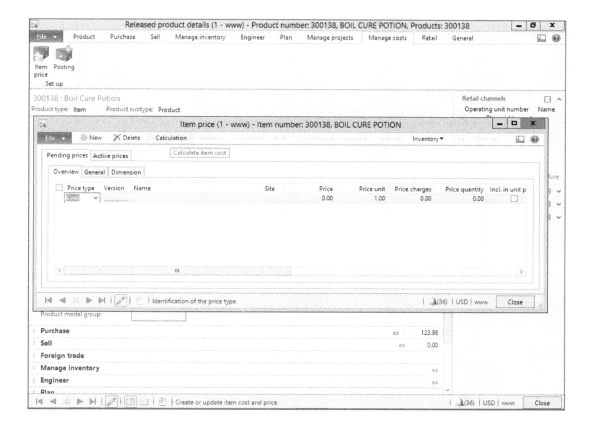

When the **Item Price** maintenance form is displayed, switch to the **Pending Prices** tab and then click on the **Calculation** button within the menu bar to start your cost rollup process.

Performing a Manual Cost Roll Up

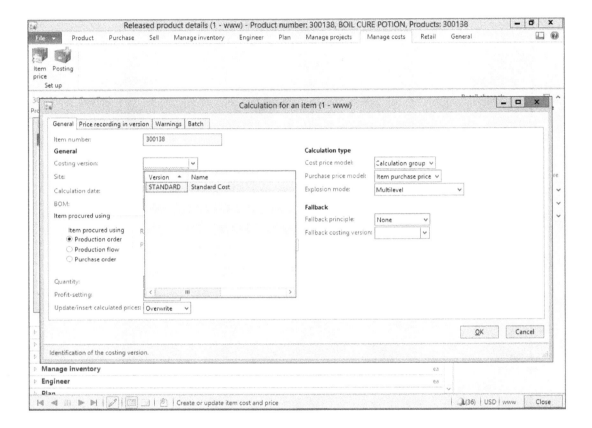

When the **Calculation for an Item** dialog box is displayed click on the **Costing Version** dropdown box, and select the costing version that you want to use for the cost roll up.

Performing a Manual Cost Roll Up

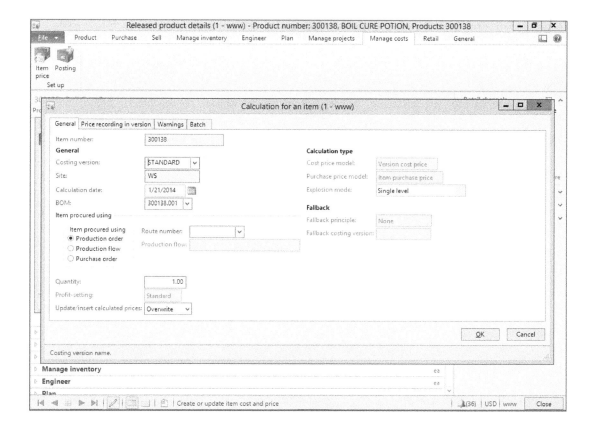

Then just click on the **OK** button to perform the cost rollup.

Performing a Manual Cost Roll Up

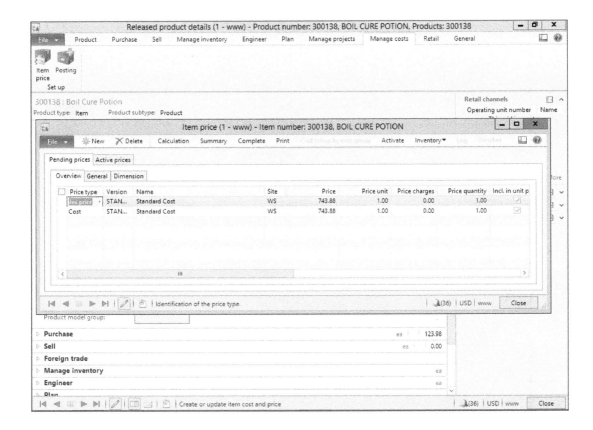

After the cost rollup is complete, then you should see a number of entries in the **Pending Prices** tab of the **Item Price** maintenance form.

Viewing Cost Rollup Details

Once you have performed a cost rollup against a product, you can drill into the cost detail to get a better idea of what all of the component costs are.

In this section we will show how you can view the cost details of a BOM.

Viewing Cost Rollup Details

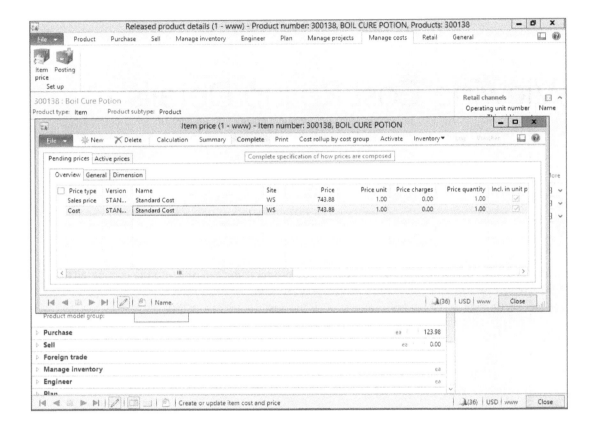

If you want to see more detailed analysis of the cost and the components, then return to the **Item Price** maintenance form and click on the **Complete** button within the menu bar.

Viewing Cost Rollup Details

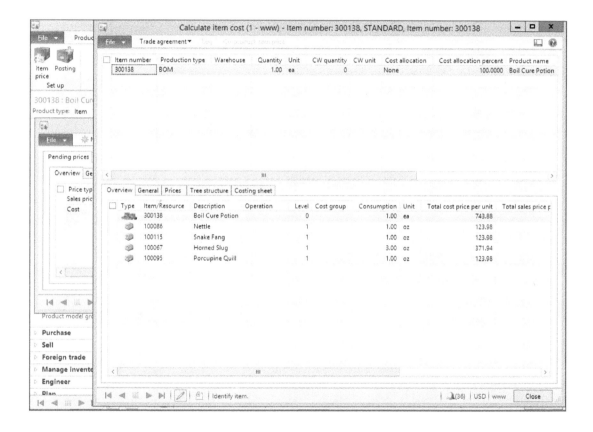

When the **Calculate Item Cost** inquiry form is shown you will be able to see all of the individual component products, and also the component cost based on the quantity that has been allocated to the BOM lines.

Activating Item Price Costs

After you have calculated your product costs, and are happy with the results, then you can activate the price so that it becomes the new standard cost of the product.

In this section we will show how to activate a pending item cost.

Activating Item Price Costs

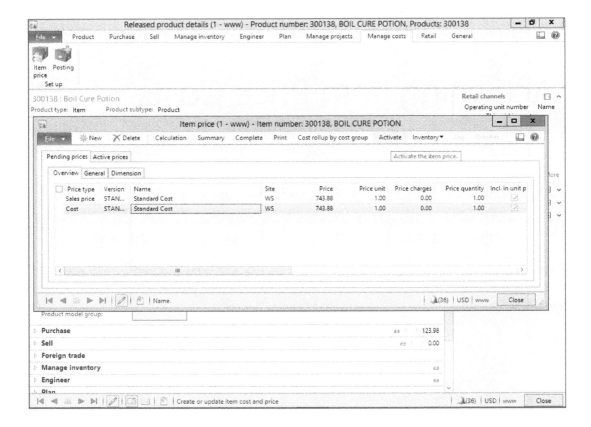

From the **Item Price** maintenance form, select the cost that you would like to activate, and then click on the **Activate** button within the menu bar.

Activating Item Price Costs

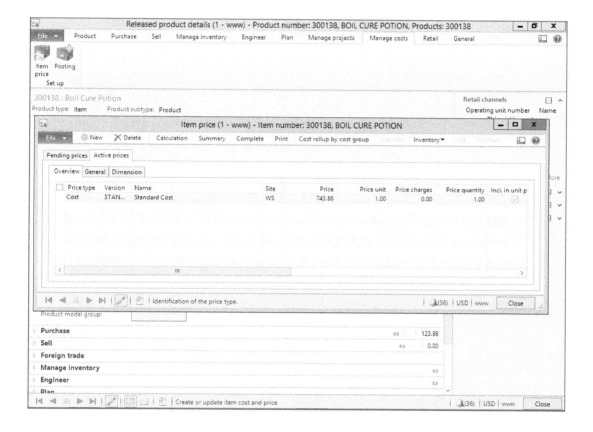

Now when you look at the process within the **Active Prices** tab of the **Item Prices** maintenance form, you should see that your cost is showing.

You can now click the **Close** button to exit from the form.

Creating a Production Order

Once you have created your Bill of Material for your product you can start using it within production. The first step in the process though it to create the **Production Job**.

Creating a Production Order

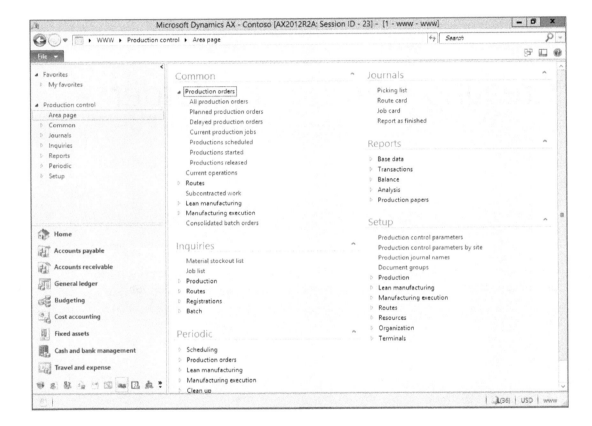

To create a new **Production Job**, click on the **All Production Orders** menu item within the **Production Orders** folder of the **Common** group of the **Production Control** area page.

Creating a Production Order

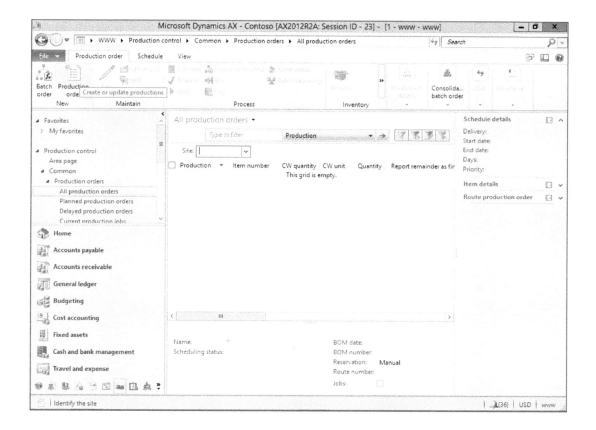

When the **Production Orders** is displayed, click on the **Production Order** button within the **New** group of the **Production Order** ribbon bar.

Creating a Production Order

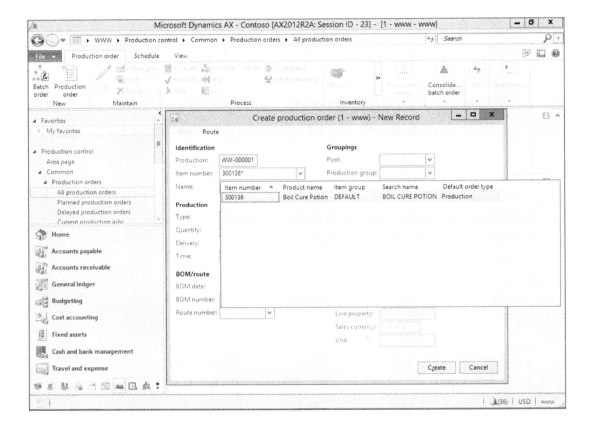

When the **Create Production Order** dialog box is displayed, select the **Item Number** that you want to start the production order for from the dropdown list.

Creating a Production Order

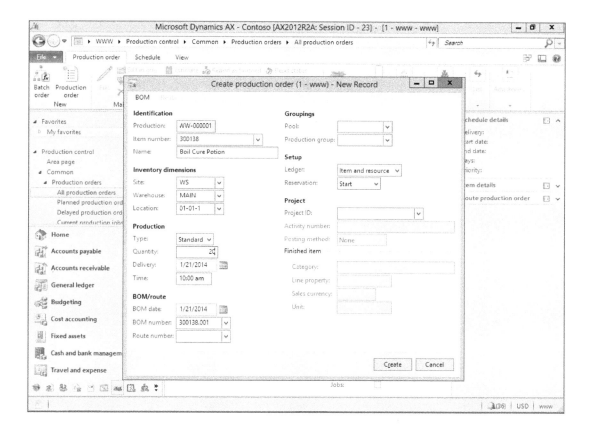

This will default in all of the **Site**, **Warehouse** and **Location** information for you and also default in the default **BOM** number. All that you need to do is specify the **Quantity** that you want to produce.

Creating a Production Order

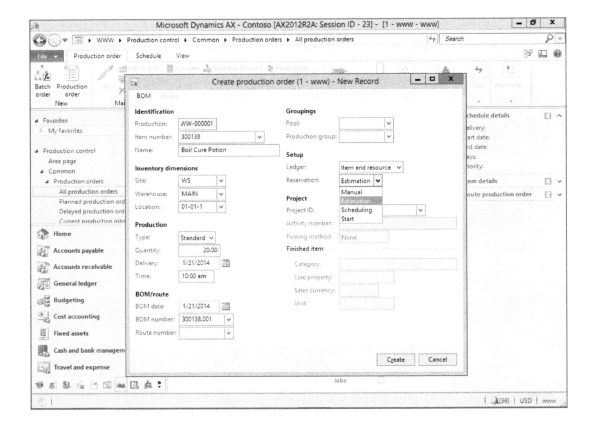

The only other tweak that you may want to make to your **Production Order** is to select the **Reservation** stage that you want to allocate the inventory at.

Creating a Production Order

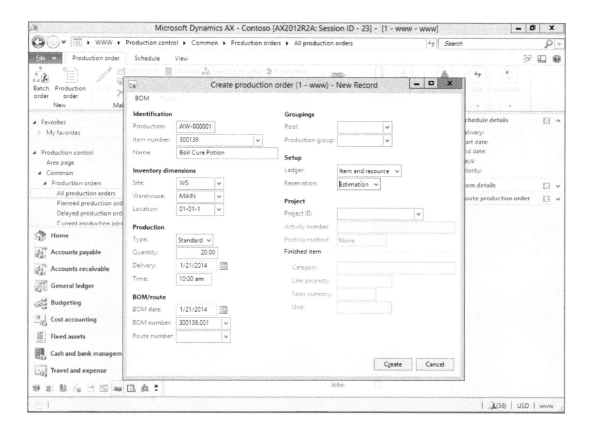

After you have configured your production order, just click on the **Create** button to create your production order.

Creating a Production Order

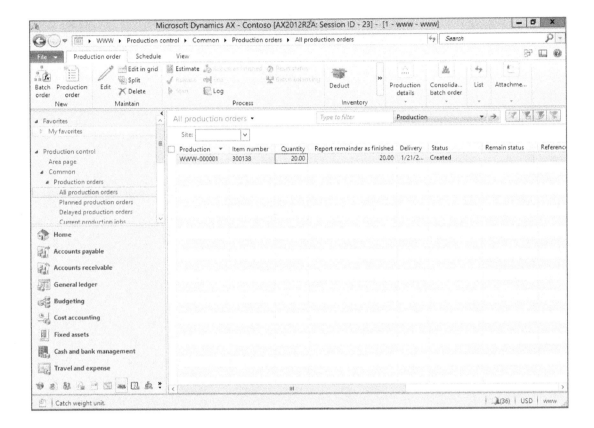

When you return back to the **All Production Orders** list page you will see that there is a new production order waiting for you to start working on.

Releasing Jobs To Production For Estimation

Once you have a **Production Order** you can firm it up and release it to production at any time for estimation, which based on your **Reservation** selection may reserve your inventory to the production order.

Releasing Jobs To Production For Estimation

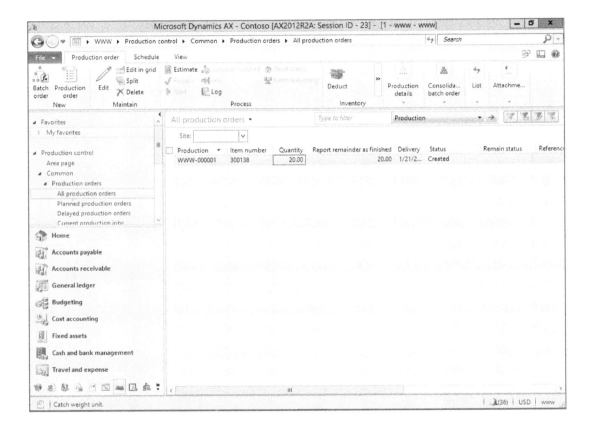

On the **All Production** Orders list page, select the production order that you want to release to production for estimation, and then click on the **Estimate** menu button within the **Process** group of the **Production Order** ribbon bar.

Releasing Jobs To Production For Estimation

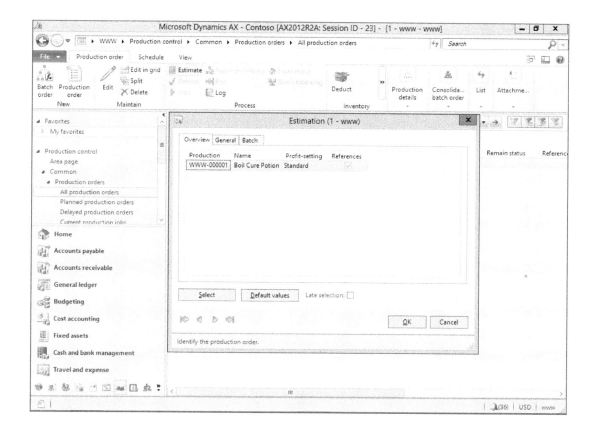

When the **Estimation** dialog box is displayed, click on the **OK** button to process the production order.

Releasing Jobs To Production For Estimation

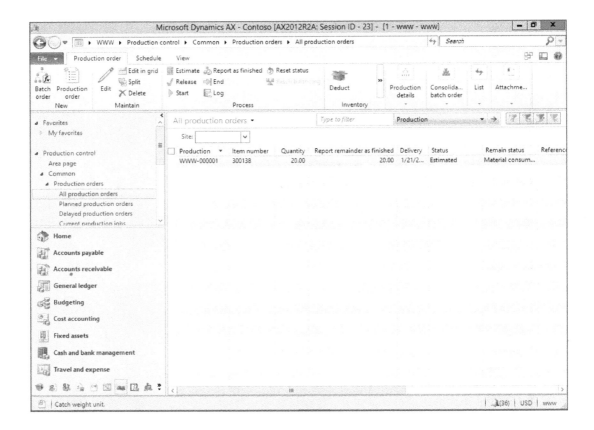

Now when you return to the **All Production Orders** list page you will notice that your production order now has a status of **Estimated** and also all of the other icons within the **Process** group of the **Production Order** ribbon bar have been enabled, allowing you now to perform more stages of the production order.

Starting Production Jobs

Once a production order has been released to production, you can officially start the job and start recording actual time and materials against the job.

Starting Production Jobs

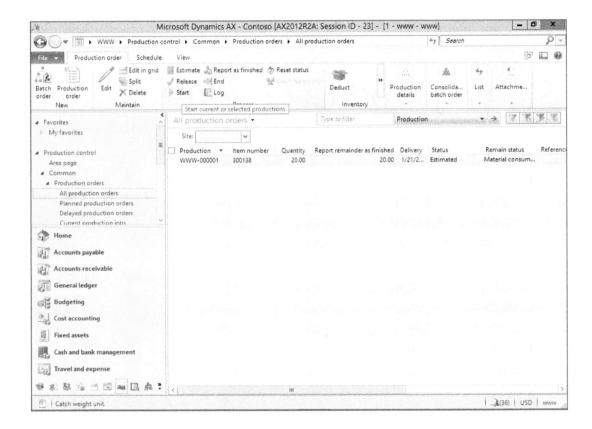

On the **All Production** Orders list page, select the production order that you want to release to production for estimation, and then click on the **Start** menu button within the **Process** group of the **Production Order** ribbon bar.

Starting Production Jobs

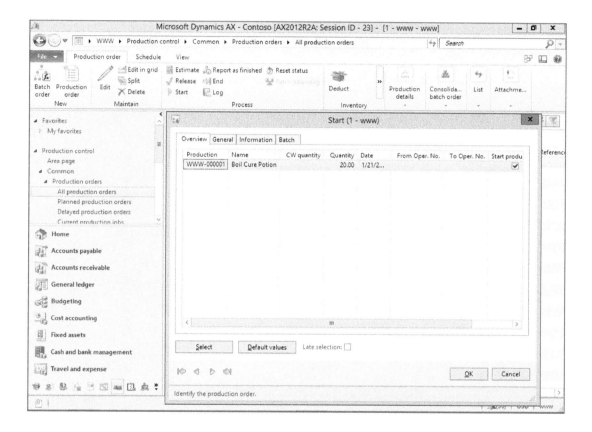

When the **Start** dialog box is displayed, click on the **OK** button to process the production order.

Note: Later on when you configure a route against your job, you will be able to select the **From Operation No** and **To Operation No** to start only certain route steps.

Starting Production Jobs

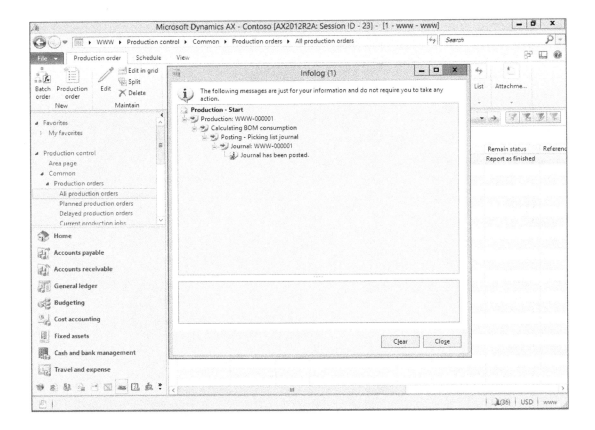

You will then get a message saying that the production orders have been created and also that the pick tickets have been created as well.

Reporting Jobs As Finished

As you process your **Production Order** you will indicate that inventory has been created by performing a **Report As Finished** transaction. You can do this at the end of the production order, or multiple times throughout the production.

Reporting Jobs As Finished

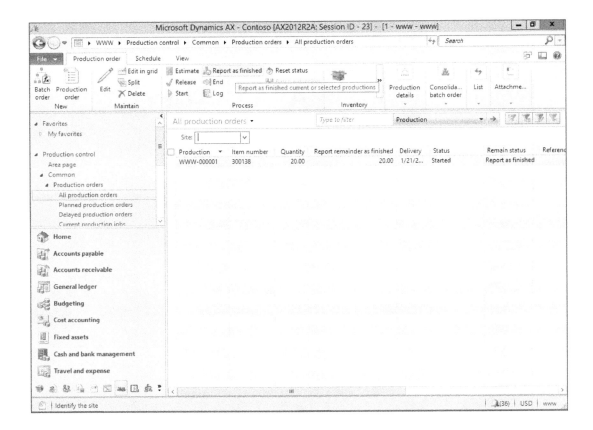

On the **All Production** Orders list page, select the production order that you want to release to production for estimation, and then click on the **Report As Finished** menu button within the **Process** group of the **Production Order** ribbon bar.

Reporting Jobs As Finished

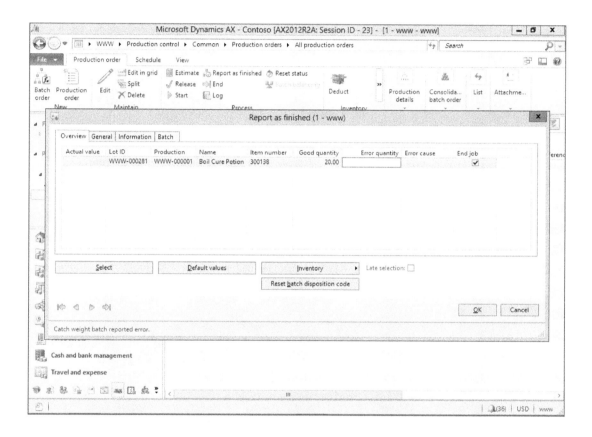

When the **Report As Finished** dialog box is displayed, enter in the **Good Quantity** and **Error Quantity**, and then click on the **OK** button to report the production.

Reporting Jobs As Finished

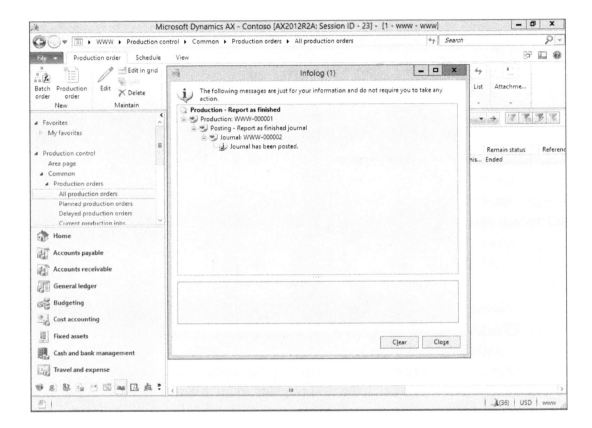

In return, **Dynamics AX** will tell you that the journals have been reported and posted.

Ending Jobs

After you have reported all of your production you can finish it and allow Dynamics AX to tidy up all of the final costs and postings by Ending the job.

Ending Jobs

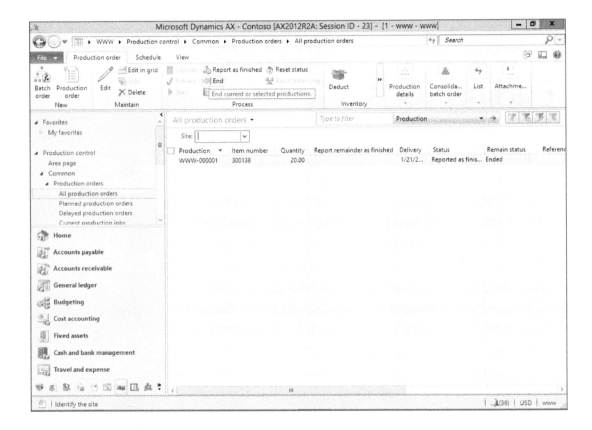

On the **All Production** Orders list page, select the production order that you want to release to production for estimation, and then click on the **End** menu button within the **Process** group of the **Production Order** ribbon bar.

Ending Jobs

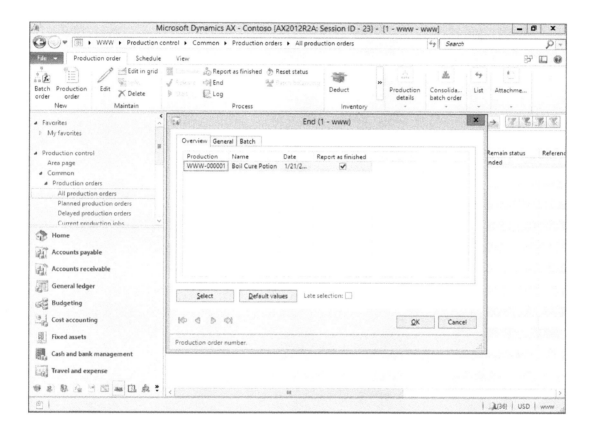

When the **End** dialog box is displayed, click on the **OK** button to process the production order.

Ending Jobs

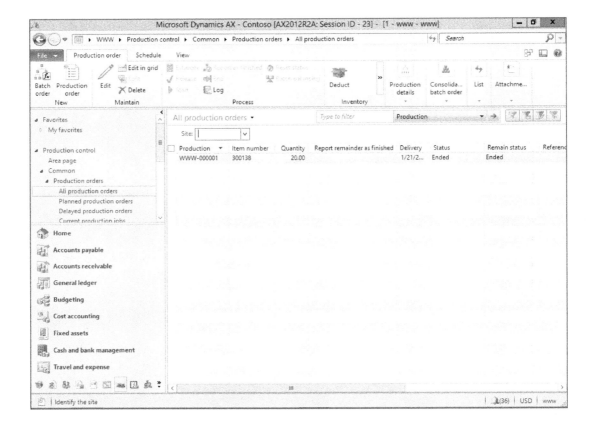

When you return to the **All Production Orders** list page you will see that your production order is in the **Ended** status, and also you can no-longer access any of the other icons within the **Process** group of the **Production Control** ribbon bar.

Tracing Job Transactions

As you are reporting all of the production and issuing raw materials to your production, Dynamics AX is tracking all of the detail behind the scenes for you. This allows you then to go back to you inventory, and perform a trace to see how any product was created, and also see all history around the product's production.

Tracing Job Transactions

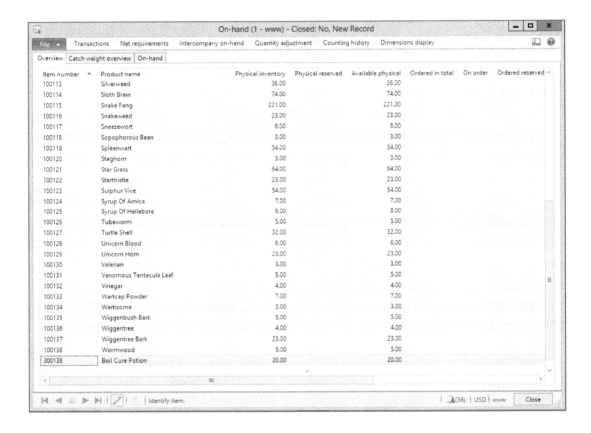

One way to view the transaction history is to start from the **On-Hand** inventory inquiry.

You just have to select the inventory that you are interested in, and then clickon the **Transactions** button in the menu bar.

Tracing Job Transactions

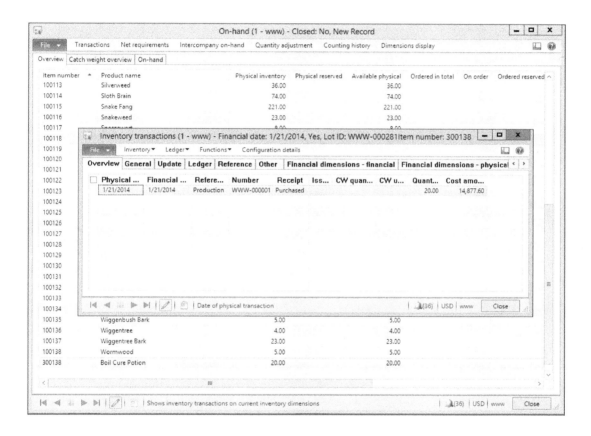

All of the inventory movements associated with the product will then be listed, including any production orders that were used to create the product.

Tracing Job Transactions

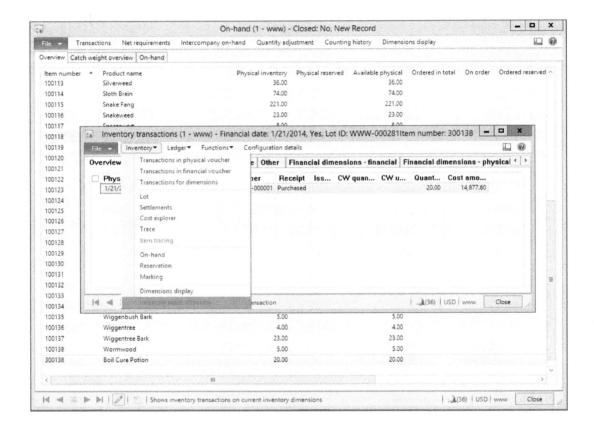

To view the inventory trace, click on the **Inventory** menu button in the menu bar, and select the **Trace** menu item.

Tracing Job Transactions

This will open up the **Trace Inventory Dimensions** view where you can expand out the trace and view all of the individual steps back to the origin.

CONFIGURING ROUTES

Once you have defined your Bills of Material for all of your products you can start getting a little more clever by creating routes for your production orders that will tell the system what resources to use during production, how long the production stages will take, and also give you more detailed costing for the product by incorporating overhead and machinery costs.

Configuring Resources

Before we start configuring our routes, we fist need to set up some resources that we will be running our production jobs through. This will allow us to also schedule by resource, and manage the capacity of the resource if we want.

Configuring Resources

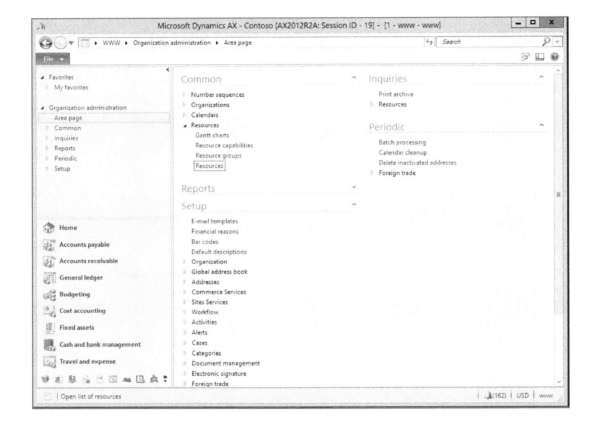

Click on the **Resources** menu item within the **Resources** folder of the **Common** group of the **Organization Administration** area page.

Configuring Resources

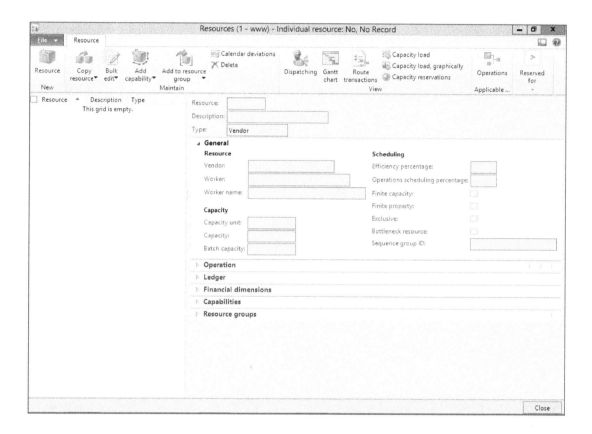

When the **Resources** maintenance form is displayed, click on the **Resource** button within the **New** group of the **Resource** ribbon bar to create a new record.

Configuring Resources

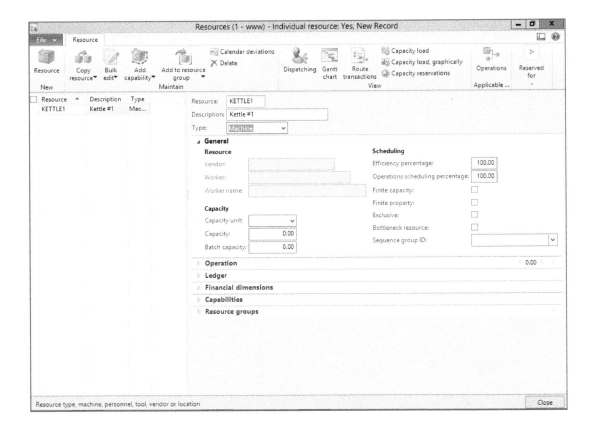

When the new record is created, assign a **Resource** code, a **Description** and also set the **Type** to be **Machine** to identify that this resource will be a piece of equipment.

Configuring Resources

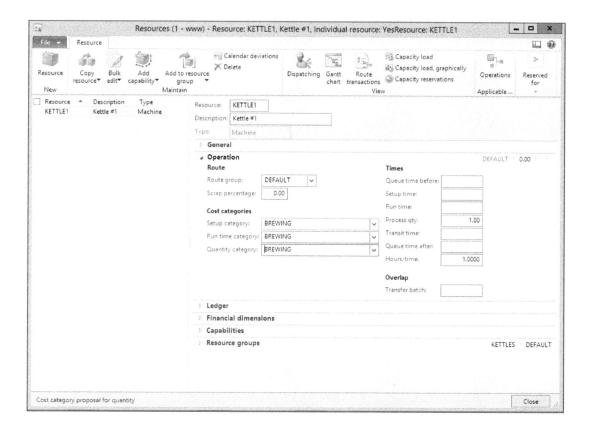

Expand the **Operation** tab on the form and set the **Route Group,** and also the Cost Categories for the **Setup Category**, the **Run-time Category**, and the **Quantity Category.**

Configuring Resources

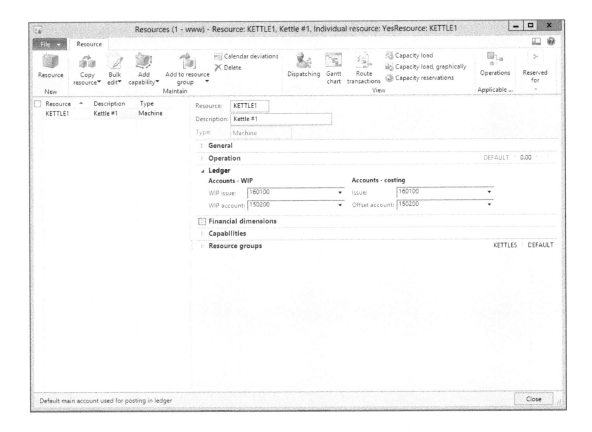

Then open up the **Ledger** tab, and configure a default accounts for **WIP** and **Costing**.

Configuring Resources

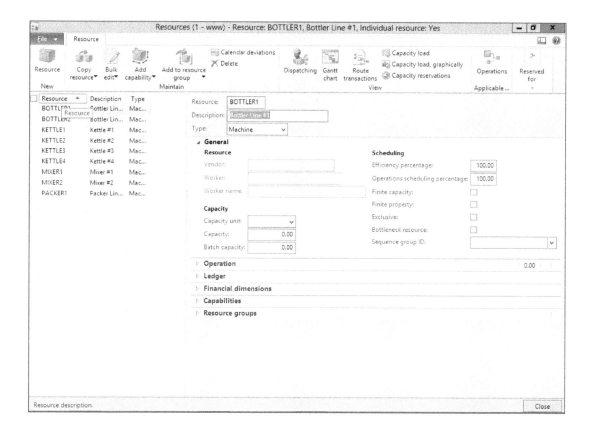

Repeat the process for all of the other resources that you want to use in your Routes, and then click the **Close** button to exit from the form.

Configuring Resource Groups

Next we will group the **Resources** by defining **Resource Groups**. This will allow us to route our operations over any of the common machines without having to list them out individually.

Configuring Resource Groups

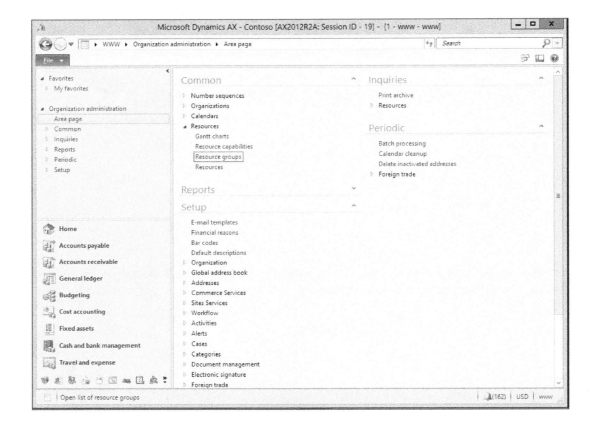

Click on the **Resource Groups** menu item within the **Resources** folder of the **Common** group within the **Organization Administration** area page.

Configuring Resource Groups

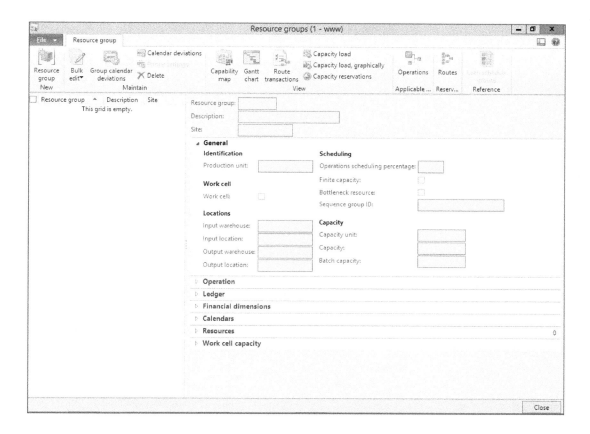

When the **Resource Group** maintenance form is displayed, click on the **Resource Group** button within the **New** group of the **Resource Group** ribbon bar.

Configuring Resource Groups

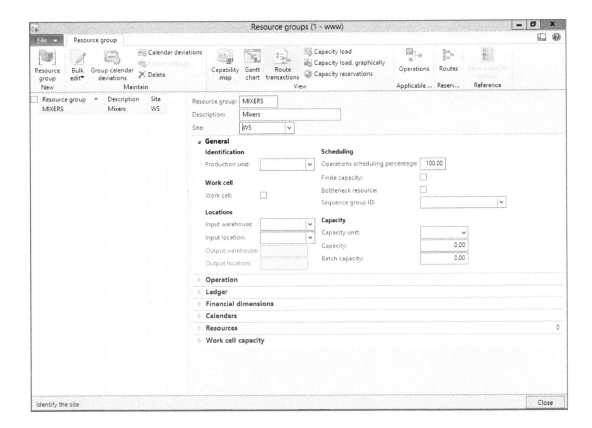

When the new record is created, assign a **Resource Group** code, a **Description** and also set select the Site that this resource group will be associated with.

Configuring Resource Groups

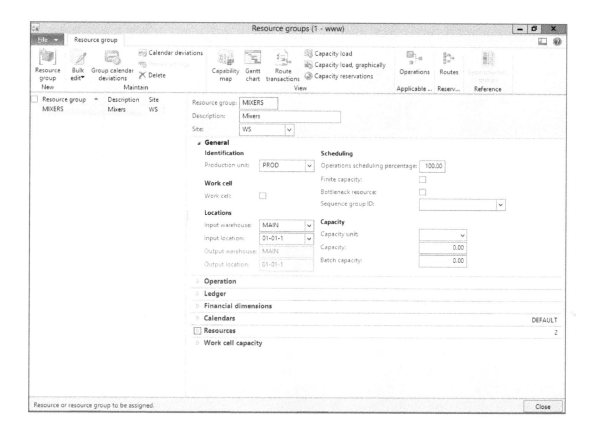

Within the **General** tab, select the **Production Unit** that this machine will be associated with. The **Production Unit** may be used to group multiple resources together as well.

Then assign a default **Input Warehouse** and **Input Location** for sourcing inventory from.

Configuring Resource Groups

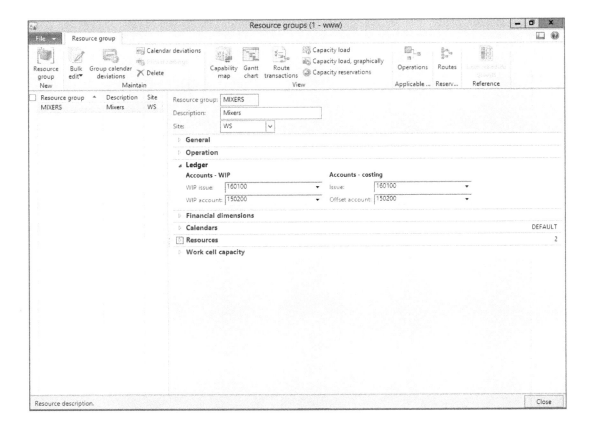

Open up the **Ledger** tab and assign your **Resource Group** some default **WIP** and **Costing** accounts.

Configuring Resource Groups

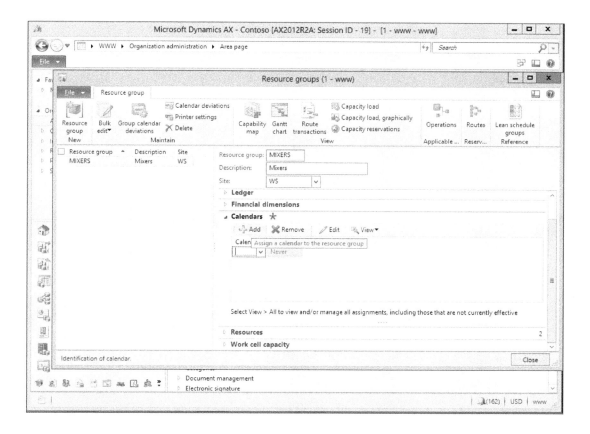

Expand the **Calendars** tab within the **Resource Groups** and click the **Add** button to insert a new Calendar record.

Configuring Resource Groups

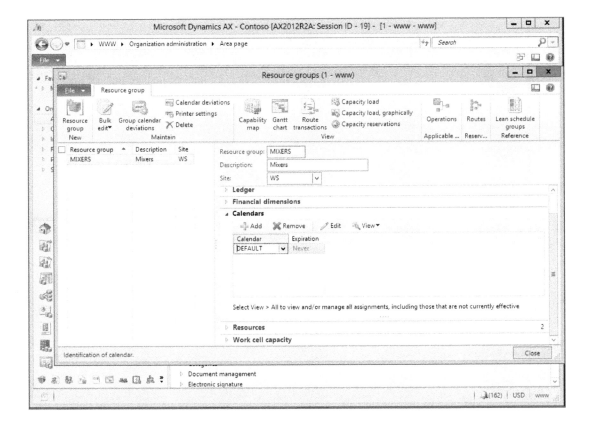

Then select the **Calendar** that you want to use to schedule the production jobs by.

Configuring Resource Groups

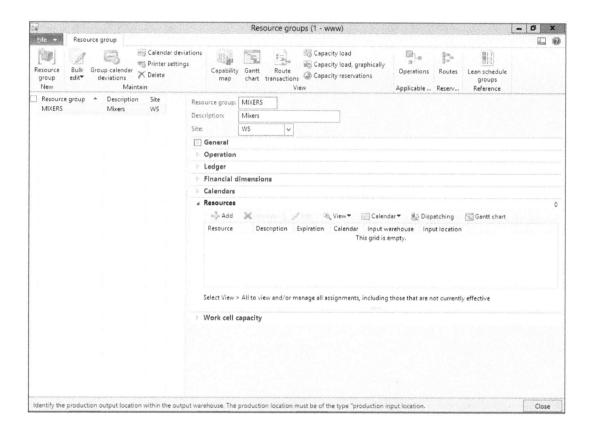

Finally, select the **Resources** tab and click on the **Add** button to create a new record.

Configuring Resource Groups

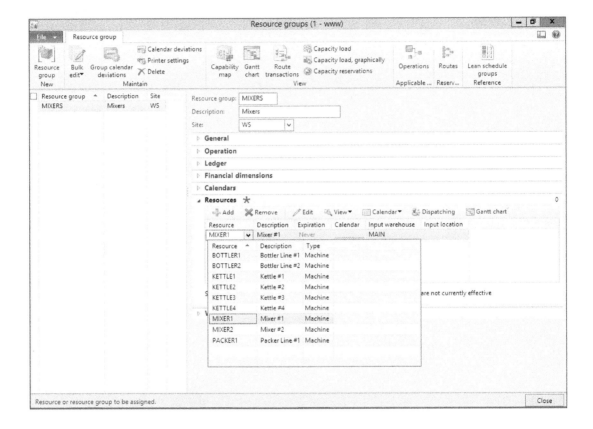

Select the **Resource** that you want to include in the **Resource Group** from the dropdown.

Configuring Resource Groups

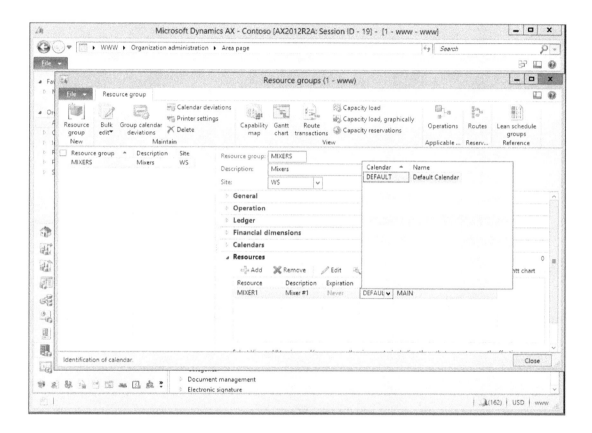

And then assign the resource a default calendar.

Configuring Resource Groups

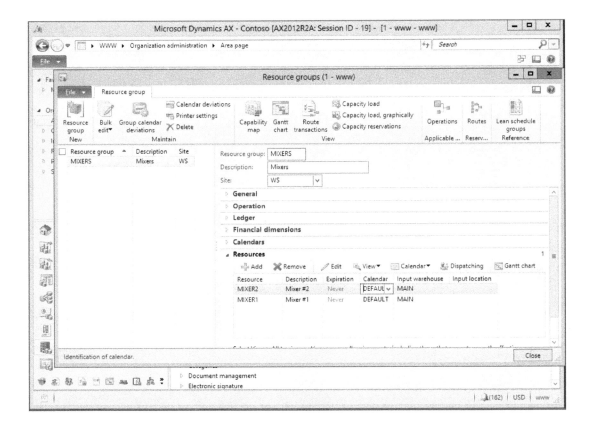

Then repeat the process to add in as many other resources that you want to use within the **Resource Group**.

Configuring Resource Groups

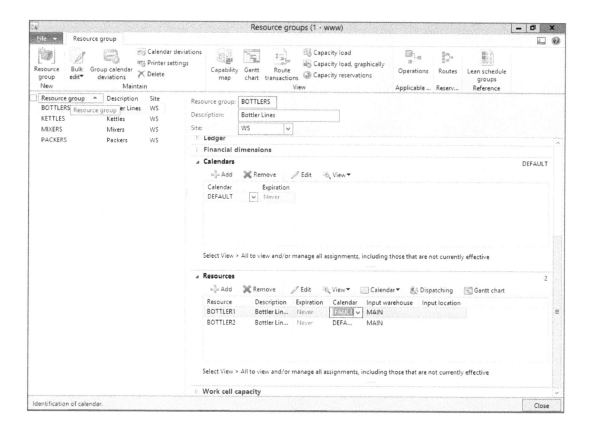

Now just repeat the setup process for all of your other **Resource Groups** and when you are done, click on the **Close** button to exit from the form.

Configuring Operations

Next we will set up the default **Operations** that will be performed within the routes. In this case, it will match up to our **Resources** but they don't have to in your case.

Configuring Operations

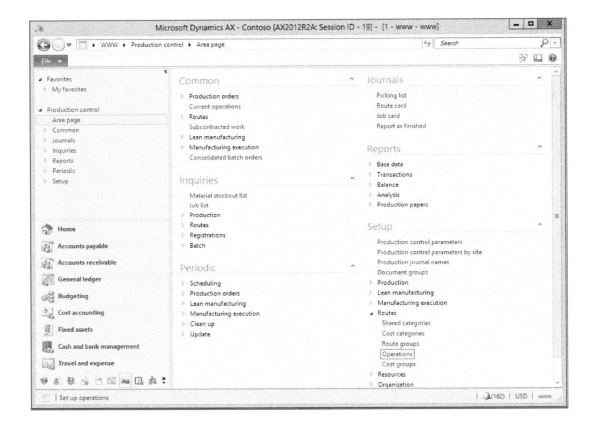

Click on the **Operations** menu item within the **Routes** folder of the **Setup** group within the **Production Control** area page.

Configuring Operations

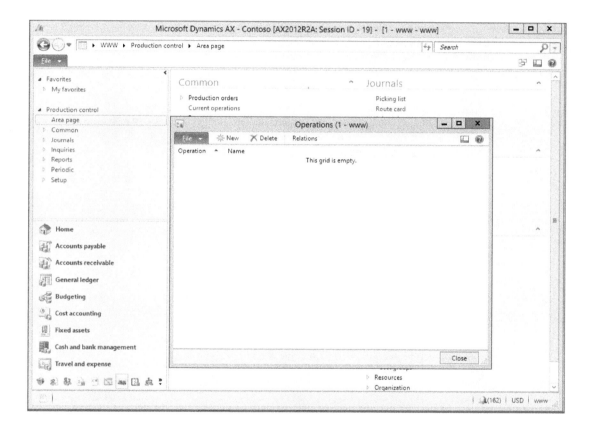

When the **Operations** maintenance form is displayed, click on the **New** button within the menu bar to create a new record.

Configuring Operations

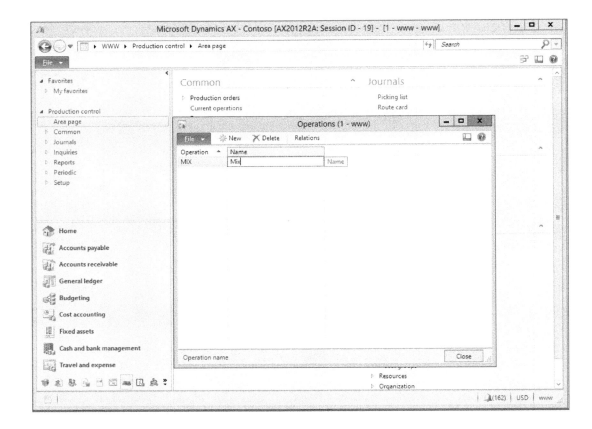

Then give your record an **Operation** code, and a **Name**.

Configuring Operations

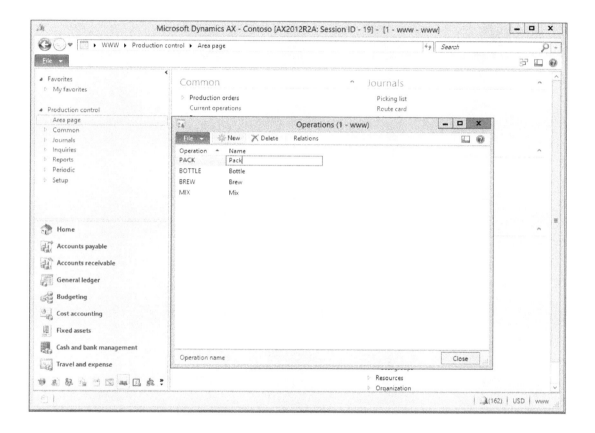

Repeat the process for all the **Operations** that you want to track within your Routes.

Configure Route Groups

Next we need to configure a **Route Group** which will be used to specify how the **Routes** will act.

Configure Route Groups

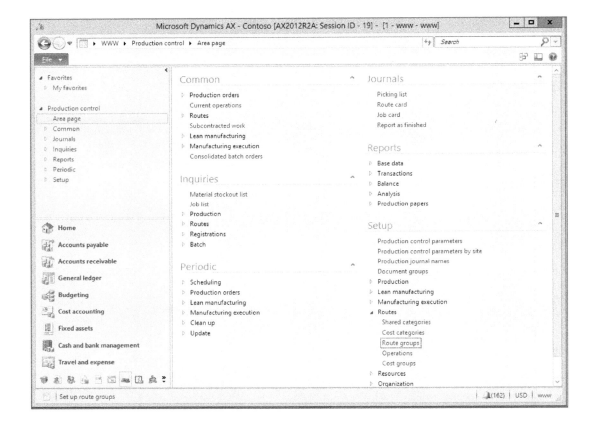

Click on the **Route Groups** menu item within the **Routes** folder of the **Setup** group within the **Production Control** area page.

Configure Route Groups

Next we need to configure a **Route Group** which will be used to specify how the **Routes** will act.

Configure Route Groups

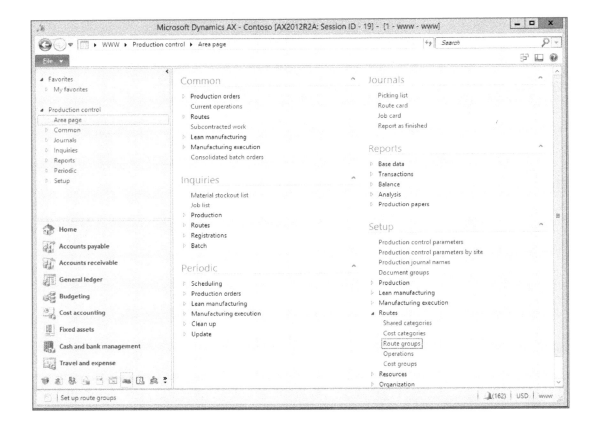

Click on the **Route Groups** menu item within the **Routes** folder of the **Setup** group within the **Production Control** area page.

Configure Route Groups

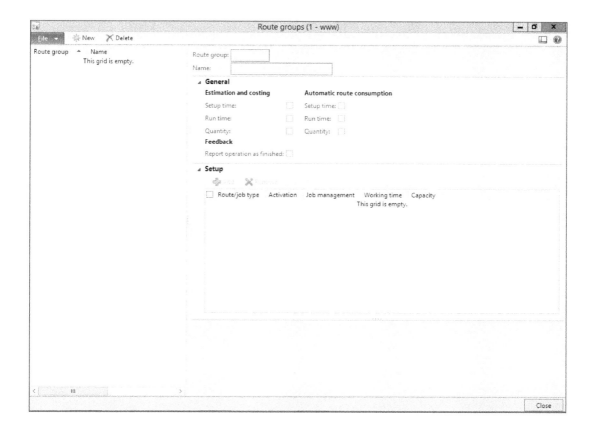

When the **Route Groups** area page is displayed, click on the **New** button to create a new record.

Configure Route Groups

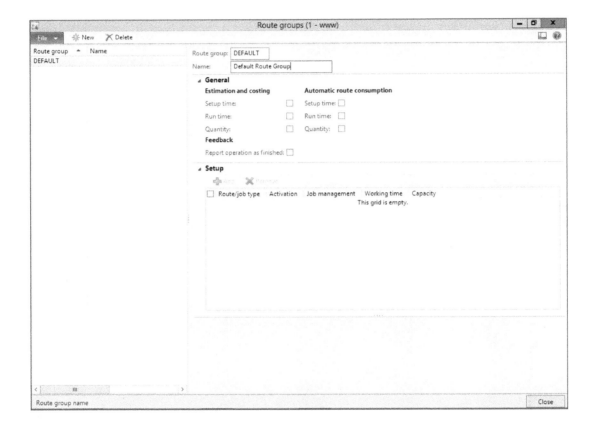

Assign the new record a **Route Group** code and a **Name**.

Configure Route Groups

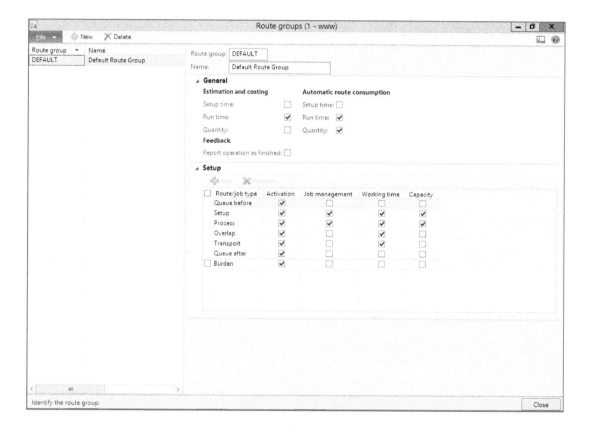

Check the **Run Time** flag within the **Estimation and Costing** group of the **General** tab to identify that only the run time will be taken into account for costing and estimating – you can tweak the other check boxes if you like.

Also check the **Run Time** and **Quantity** flags within the **Automatic Route Consumption** group to indicate that you will automatically backflush the time and material for production.

Finally make sure the **Setup** configuration looks something like the example that we have here.

When you are done, click on the **Close** button to exit from the form.

Configure Shared Categories

We are nearly set up to start building our Route. The last thing that we need to configure are the **Cost Categories**, but before we can set up those we need to configure the **Shared Category** details for the **production Cost Categories** which will be used to create them.

Configure Shared Categories

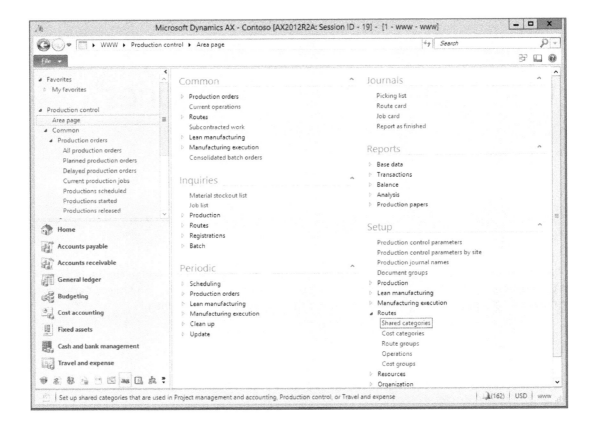

Click on the **Shared Categories** menu link within the **Routes** folder of the **Setup** group of the **Production Control** area page.

Configure Shared Categories

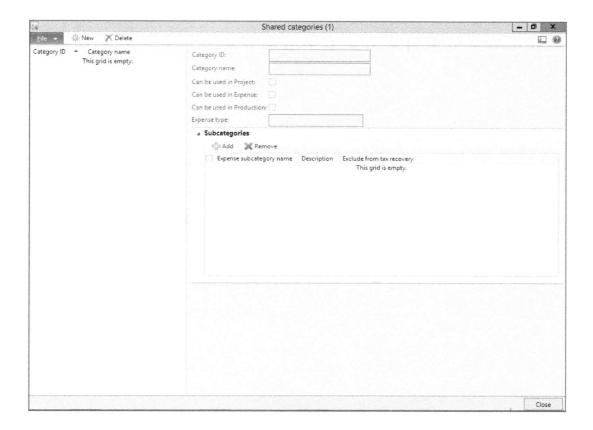

When the **Shared Categories** maintenance form is displayed, click on the **New** button within the menu bar to create a new record.

Configure Shared Categories

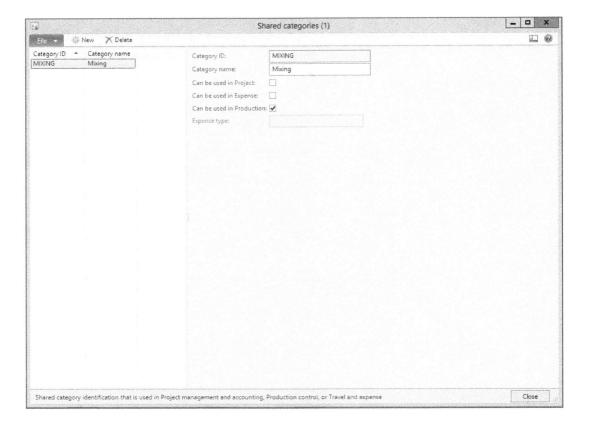

Then assign the record a **Category ID** code, and a **Category Name**.

Also, make sure that you check the **Can Be Used In Production** checkbox, otherwise you will not be able to use it within production.

Configure Shared Categories

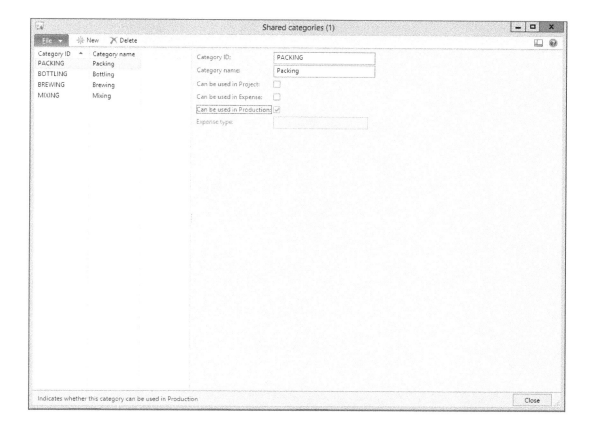

Repeat the process for all of the other **Shared Categories** that you want to track within you **Cost Categories** and then click the **Close** button to exit the form.

Configure Cost Categories

The final step is to define your **Cost Categories** that you will be using within the **Routes**. These are used to tell the system where to post all of the costs, and also allow you to set up standard costs for your resources based on run times etc.

Configure Cost Categories

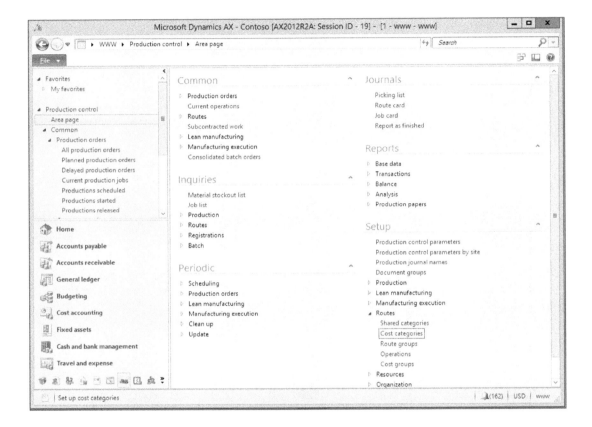

Click on the **Cost Categories** menu item within the **Routes** folder of the **Setup** group within the **Production Control** area page.

Configure Cost Categories

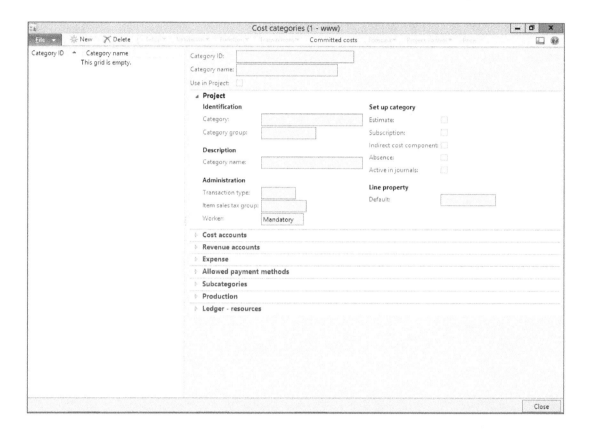

When the **Cost Categories** maintenance form is displayed, click on the **New** button within the menu bar to create a new record.

Configure Cost Categories

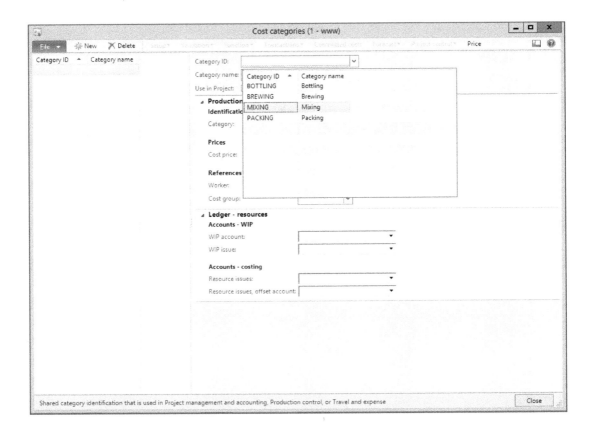

Select the **Shared Category** that you want to use from the **Category ID** dropdown list.

Configure Cost Categories

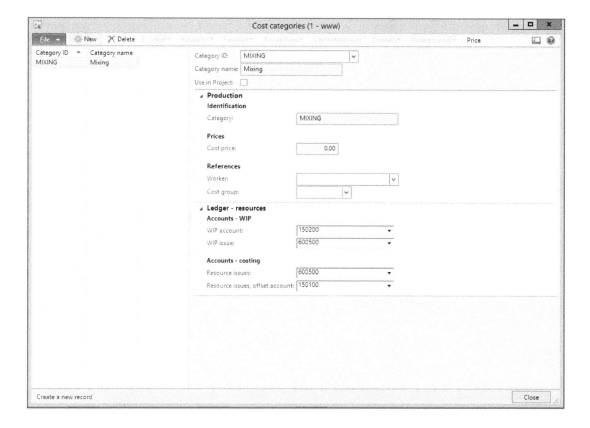

Then set the default **Ledger** accounts for the **Cost Category.**

Configure Cost Categories

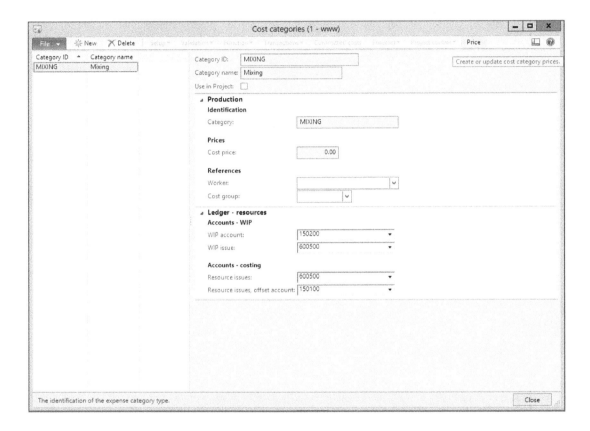

Now click on the **Price** menu item within the menu bar to allow us to specify the standard costs for our **Cost Category.**

Configure Cost Categories

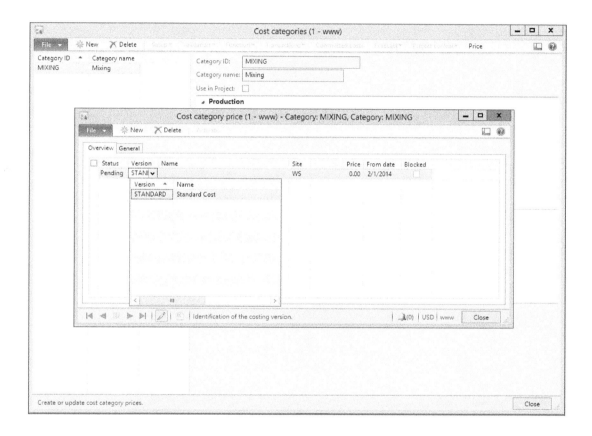

When the **Cost Category Prices** maintenance form is displayed, click on the **New** button to create a new record and then select the **Costing Version** that you want to use from the **Version** dropdown list.

Configure Cost Categories

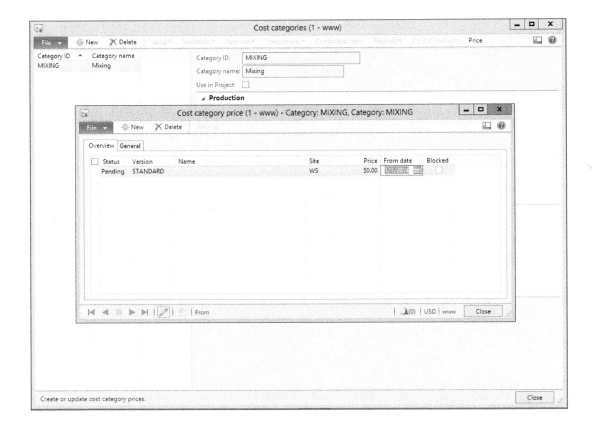

Then set the **Price** of that resource and add a **From Date**.

Configure Cost Categories

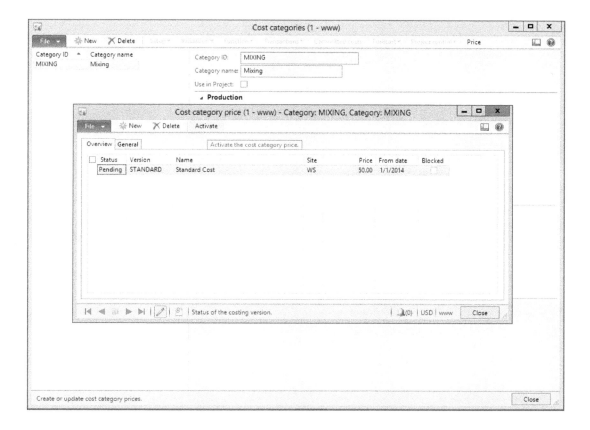

Save the records (**CTRL+S**) and the **Activate** menu item should become enabled, and you will be able to click on it.

Configure Cost Categories

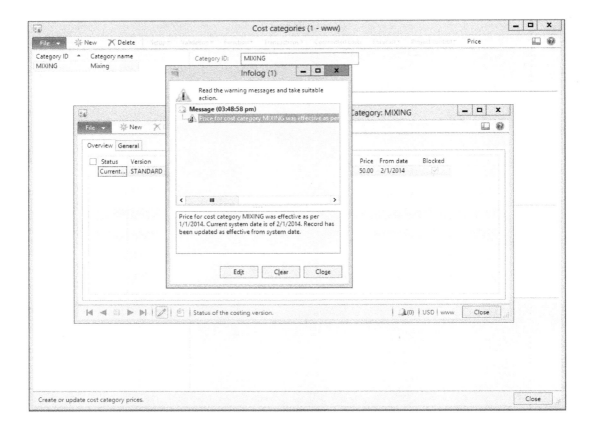

This should activate your price record against the **Cost Category**.

Configure Cost Categories

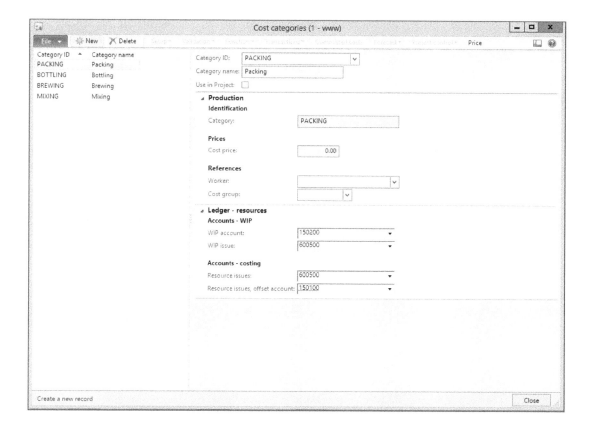

Repeat the process for all of the other **Cost Categories** and then click on the **Close** button to exit from the form.

Configuring Routes

Now that we have all of the codes and controls configured for out **Route** we can start building them.

Configuring Routes

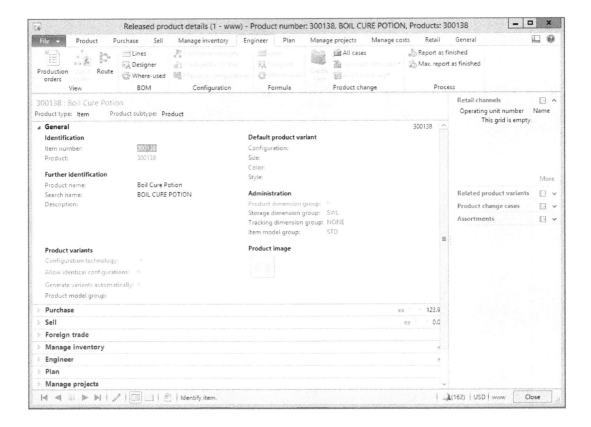

Return to your product that you configured your **Bill Of Materials** for and click on the **Route** button within the **View** group of the **Engineer** ribbon bar.

Configuring Routes

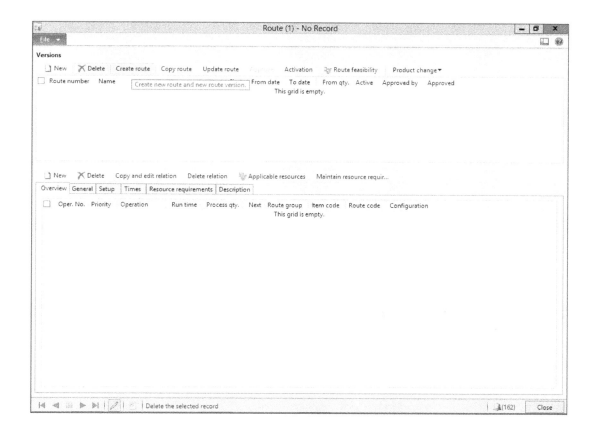

When the **Route** maintenance form is displayed, click on the **Create Route** button within the menu bar to create your first **Route** record.

Configuring Routes

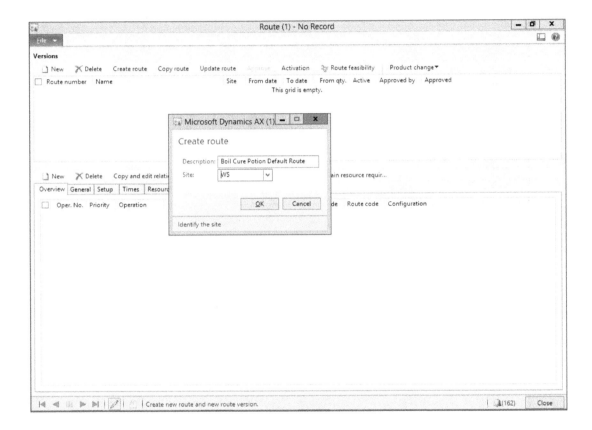

When the **Create Route** dialog box is displayed, assign you **Route** a **Description** and also set the **Site** that the **Route** will be associated. Then click on the **OK** button.

Configuring Routes

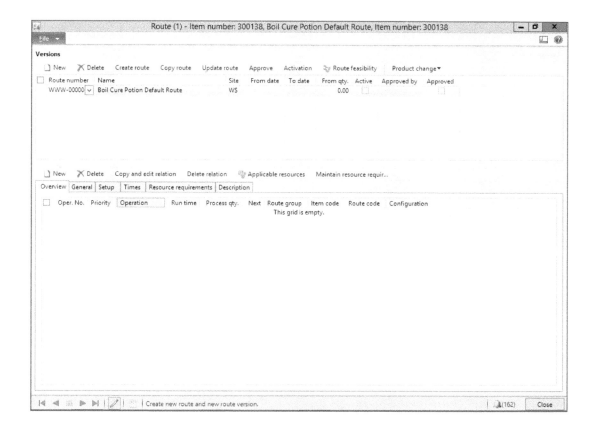

You should now have a new **Route** record. All you need to do now is add the route lines. To do that click on the **New** button within the second half of the form.

Configuring Routes

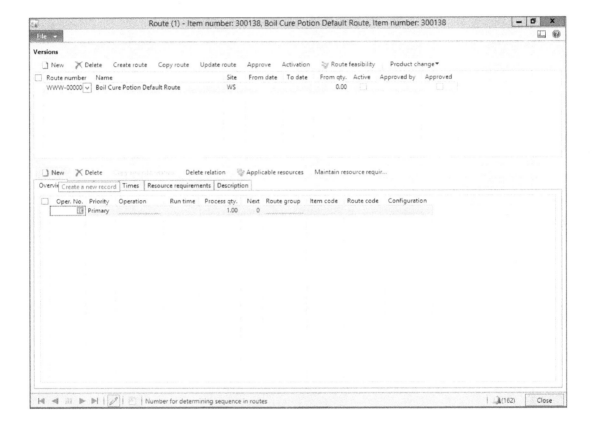

When the new **Route** operation line is created, set the **Operation No**.

Configuring Routes

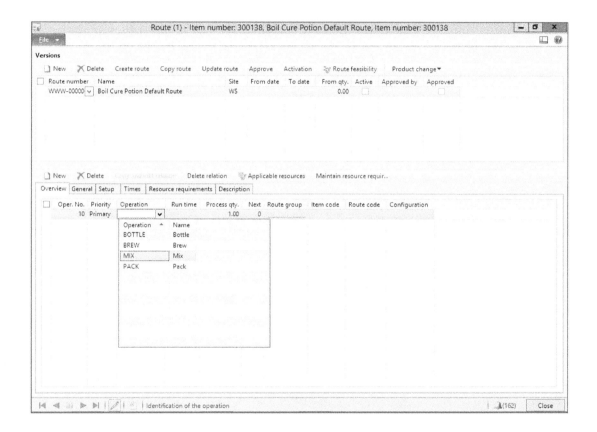

Then select the **Operation** from the dropdown list.

Configuring Routes

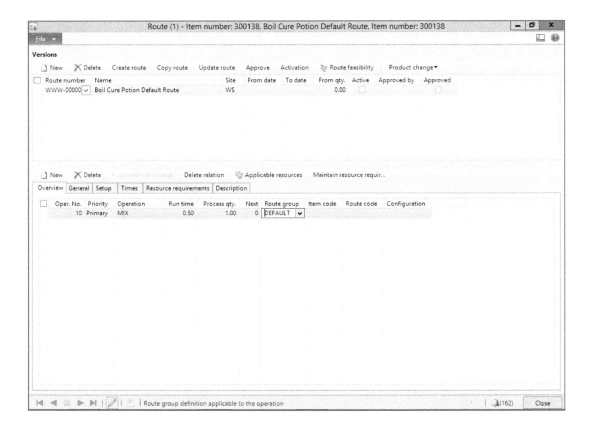

And assign the **Operation Line** a **Route Group**.

Configuring Routes

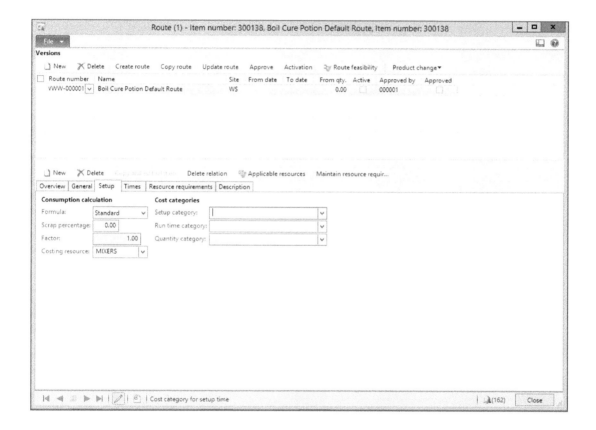

Switch the **Operation Line** tab to the **Setup** tab and set the **Costing Resource** to either a **Resource** or a **Resource Group.**.

Configuring Routes

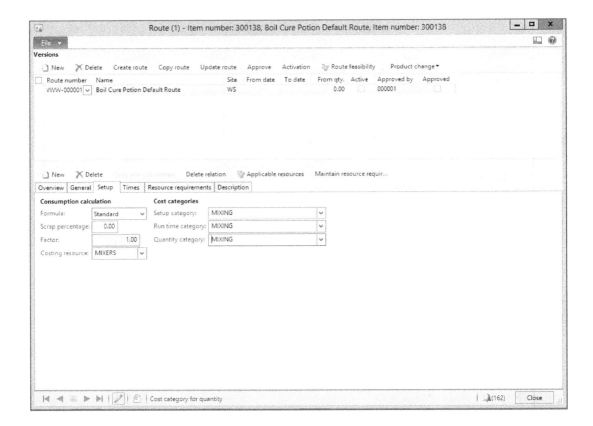

Then set the **Setup**, **Run-time**, and **Quantity** Cost Categories.

Note: if you want to be even more clever, then you can set up individual **Cost Categories** for each of these fields which would allow you to post the costs for each of these areas to different GL accounts.

Configuring Routes

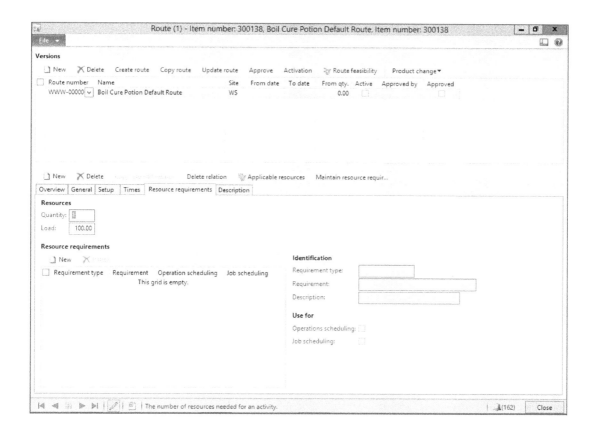

Now switch the **Operation Line** tab to the **Resource Requirements** tab.

Configuring Routes

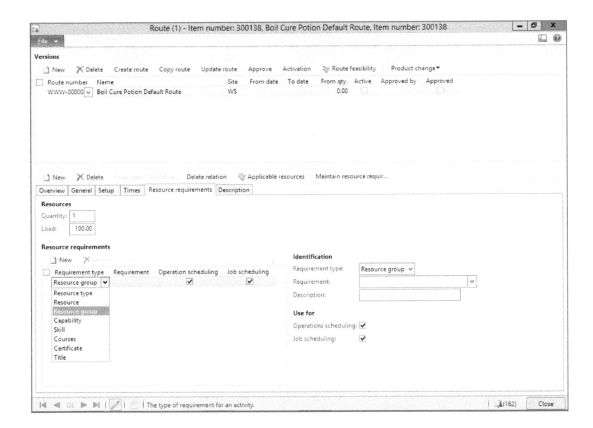

Add a new **Resource** record by clicking on the **New** menu item, and then select the type of resource that you want to use for the operation. In this case we will select the **Resource Group** option so that we can have the system schedule over all the **Resources** in the group.

Configuring Routes

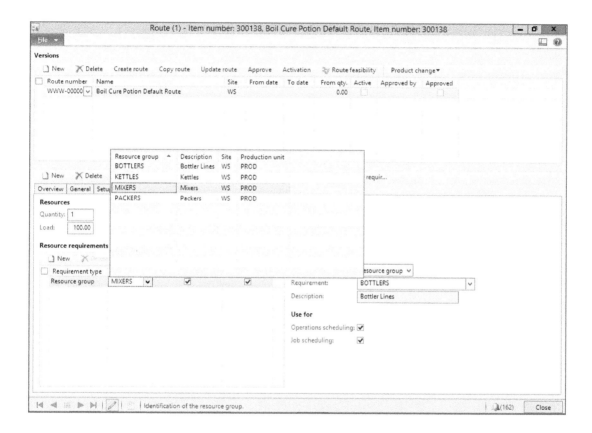

And then select the **Resource Group** that you want to use for the **Operation Line** from the **Requirement** drop down.

Configuring Routes

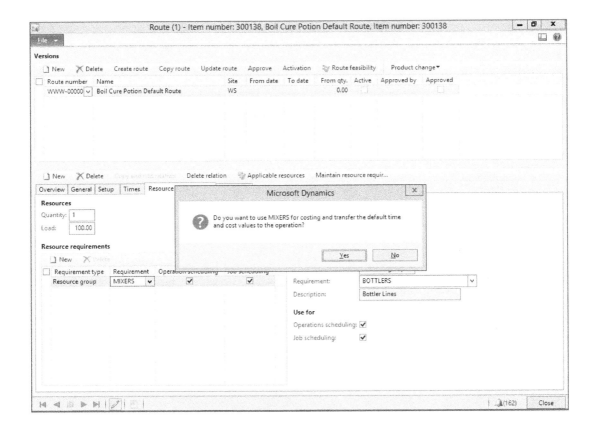

Dynamics AX will then ask you if you want to copy all of the costing information from the **Resource Group** to the **Operation Line. Click** Yes.

Configuring Routes

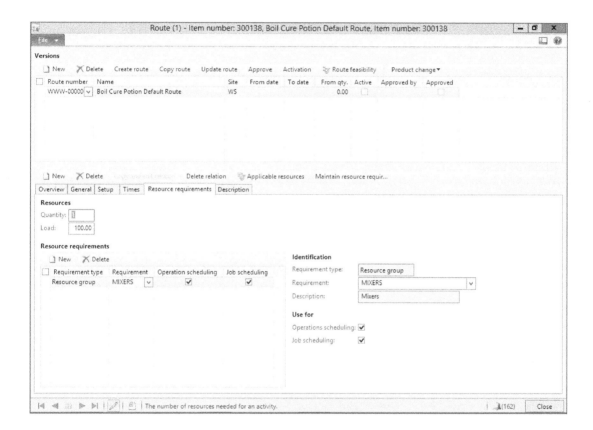

As a side note – you can associate multiple **Resource Requirements** to the **Operation Line** if you like, and by checking the **Operation Scheduling** and **Job Scheduling** flags for the resources, you are able to have the system use one resource over the other depending on the type of scheduling that you are performing.

Now you just have to set up all of the other **Operations** that you want to use in the **Route**.

Configuring Routes

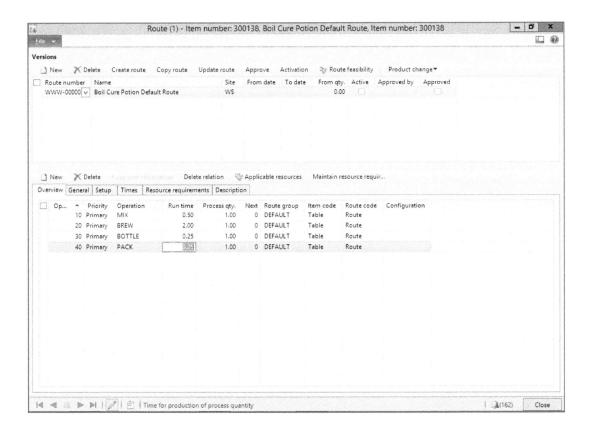

To put the finishing touches on the **Route** return to the **Overview** tab, and set all of the **Run Time** values for each step of the **Route.**

Testing Route Feasibility

If you want to perform a quick litmus test against your **Route** to see if everything is configured correctly then you can perform a **Route Feasibility** test against it. This process will quickly tell you if you have your resources configured correctly and also if all of the underlying calendars are configured correctly.

Testing Route Feasibility

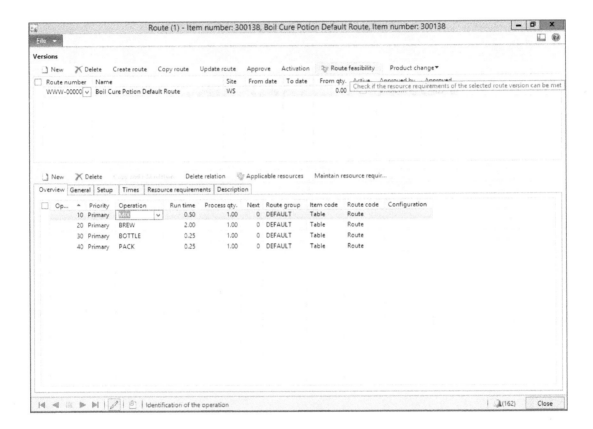

To do that, click on the **Route Feasibility** menu item within the menu bar of the **Route** maintenance form.

Testing Route Feasibility

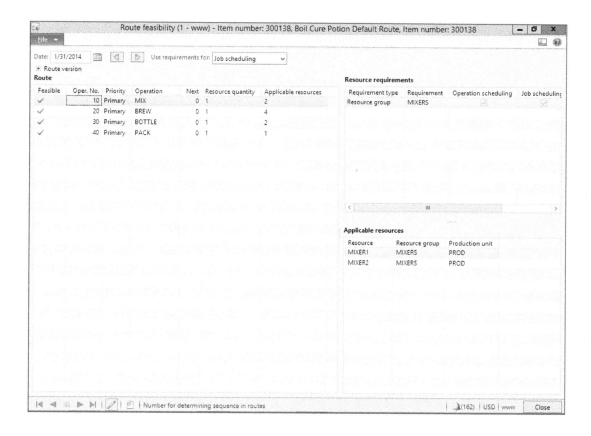

If everything is configured correctly you should see green check marks all over the place, and also all of your resources should be showing up under the right route steps.

Approving Your Route

Once you have created your **Route** and you are fairly certain that it works, you should **Approve** it so that you can start using it within your production.

Approving Your Route

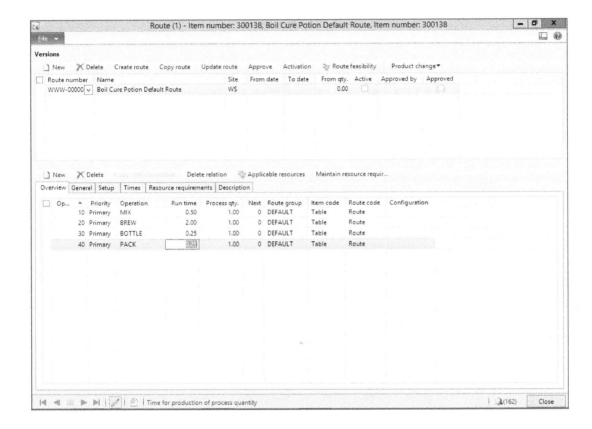

To do that, click on the **Approve** menu item within the top menu bar of the **Routes** maintenance page.

Approving Your Route

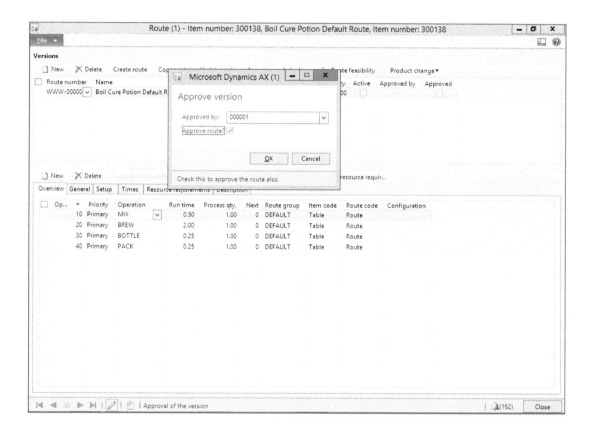

When the **Approve Version** dialog box is displayed, check the **Approve Route** check box, and then click on the **OK** button.

Approving Your Route

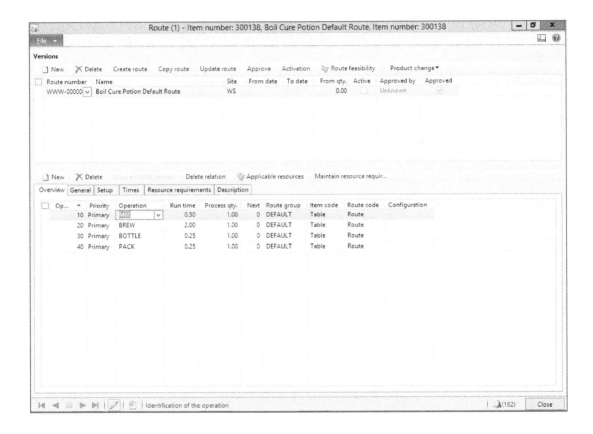

Now the **Route** should have the **Approved** check box set.

Activating Your Route

In order to make this **Route** the default **Route** that is to be used by the system you need to **Activate** it.

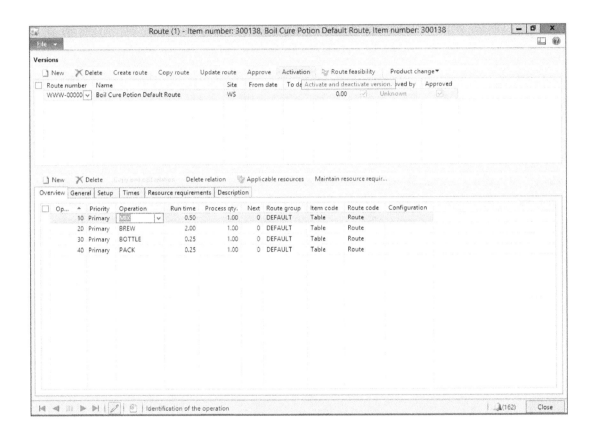

To do that, just click on the **Activation** button within the menu bar of the **Route** maintenance form. That will make the **Route** that you have currently selected the Active route for production.

Linking BOM Lines To Route Operations

Now that you have the **Route** configured, you can now link the lines in your **BOM** over to the **Route** operations. This will allow the system to know which requirements are associated with each step and also allow you to pick by **Route** step if you are so inclined.

Linking BOM Lines To Route Operations

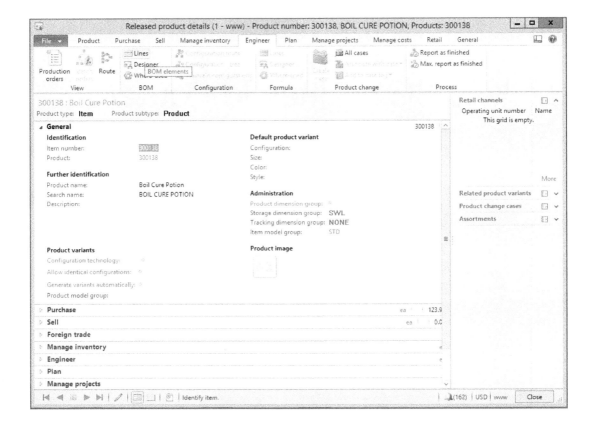

Open up the Released Product that you have been working on and access the **Bill Of Material** by clicking on the **Lines** button within the **BOM** group of the **Engineer** ribbon bar.

Linking BOM Lines To Route Operations

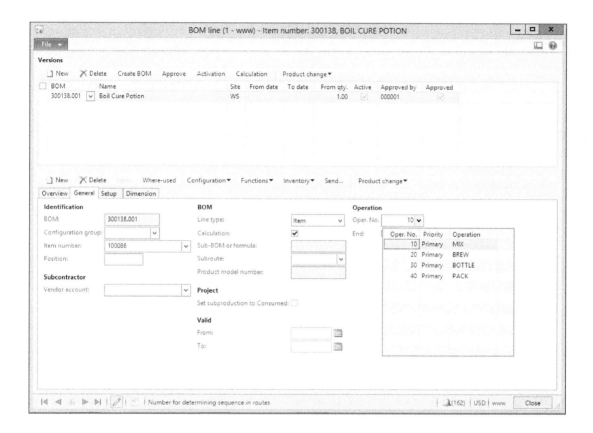

When the **BOM Line** maintenance form is displayed, select the line that you want to associate with the **Route Operation** and switch to the **General** tab.

Select the **Operation No.** from the list of **Operations** that are available in the **Route**.

Linking BOM Lines To Route Operations

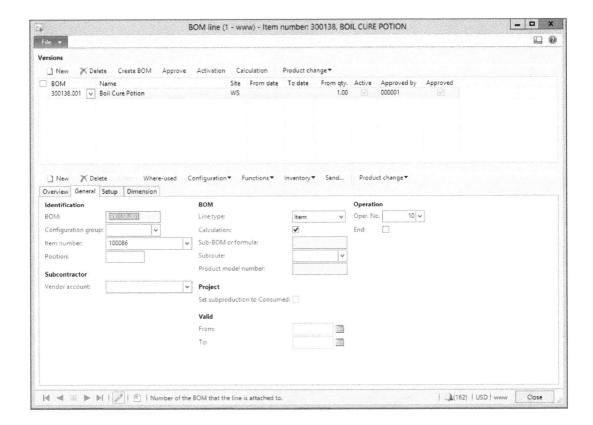

Then repeat the process for all of the other lines that are in the **BOM**.

When you are finished, just click the **Close** button to exit the form.

Performing Cost Roll Ups With Route Details

Now that we have the **Routes** configured we can start getting a little more detailed costing analysis from Dynamics AX that includes the overhead costs of the Resource operations. All we need to do is re-run the Cost Roll Up.

Performing Cost Roll Ups With Route Details

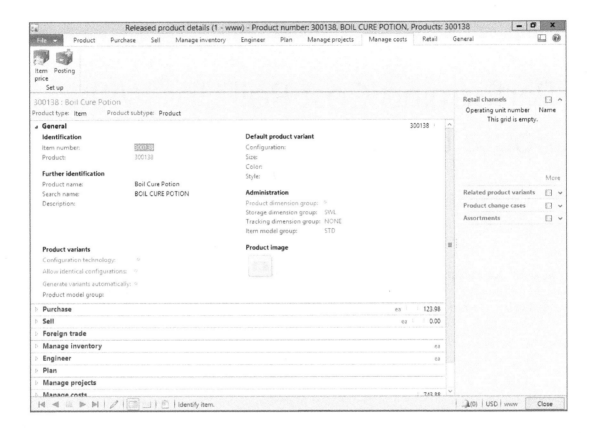

To do that, open up the product that you have been working on and click on the **Item Price** button within the **Setup** group of the **Manage Costs** ribbon bar.

Performing Cost Roll Ups With Route Details

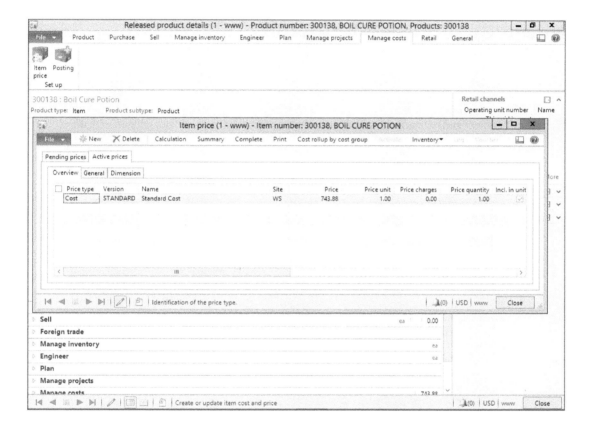

When the **Item Price** maintenance form is displayed, click on the **Calculation** menu item within the menu bar.

Performing Cost Roll Ups With Route Details

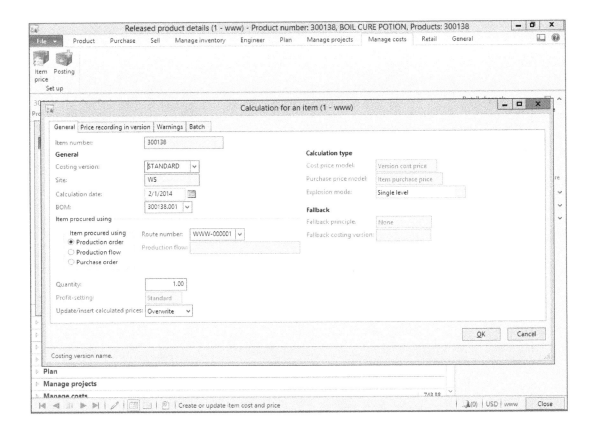

When the **Calculation For An Item** dialog box is displayed, select the **Costing Version** and then click on the **OK** button to perform the cost roll up.

Note: Notice that the currently active BOM and Route automatically default in, if you want to cost based on an alternate route or BOM, then you can easily change them here.

Performing Cost Roll Ups With Route Details

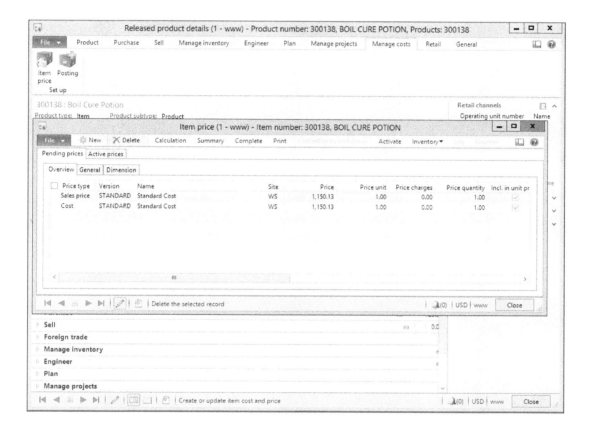

After the cost calculation has been performed, you should see all of the new cost estimates in the **Pending Prices** tab, and they should be a little higher than the original cost that did not take into account the overhead of the resources.

Performing Cost Roll Ups With Route Details

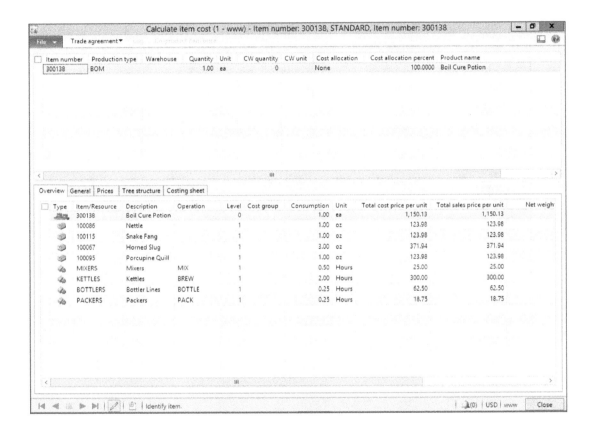

If you click on the **Complete** menu item within the **Item Price** form, you will be able to see all of the additional costs that were incurred.

Performing Cost Roll Ups With Route Details

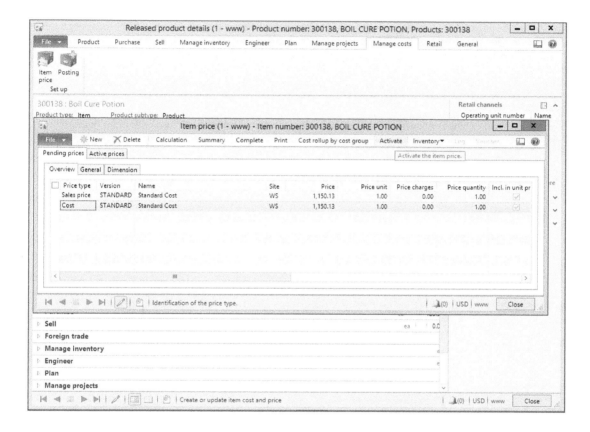

Now select the pending **Cost** price and click the **Activate** button.

Performing Cost Roll Ups With Route Details

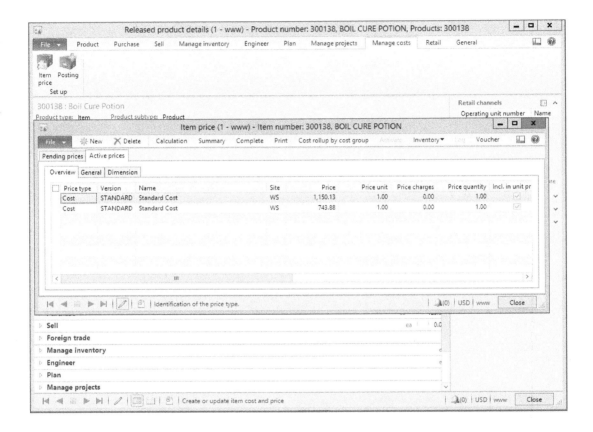

Now you will see the new price within the **Active Prices** tab of the **Item Price** form.

Creating Route Based Production Orders

Now we can start creating production jobs that are linked to **Route** operations. The process is almost exactly the same as we did earlier on with the simpler production orders.

Creating Route Based Production Orders

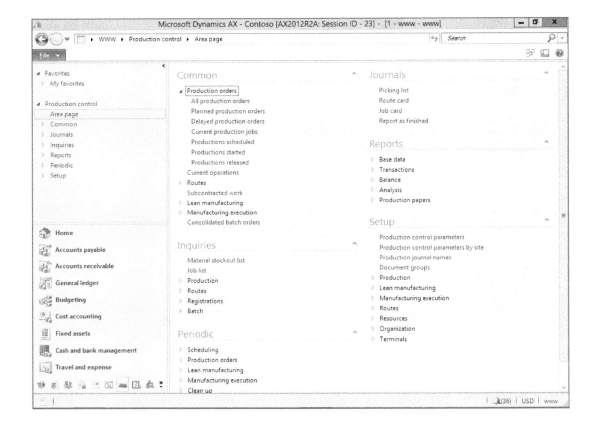

To create a new **Production Job**, click on the **All Production Orders** menu item within the **Production Orders** folder of the **Common** group of the **Production Control** area page.

Creating Route Based Production Orders

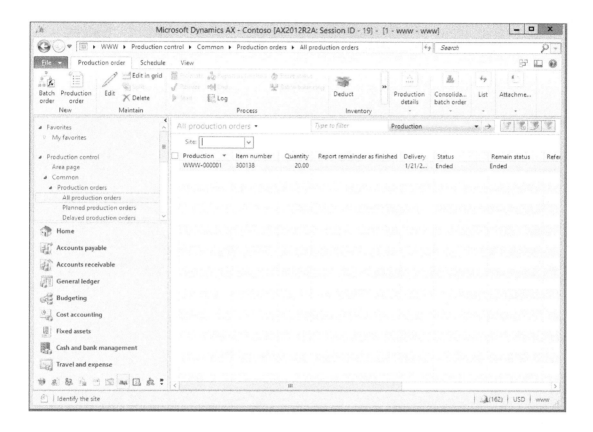

When the **Production Orders** is displayed, click on the **Production Order** button within the **New** group of the **Production Order** ribbon bar.

Creating Route Based Production Orders

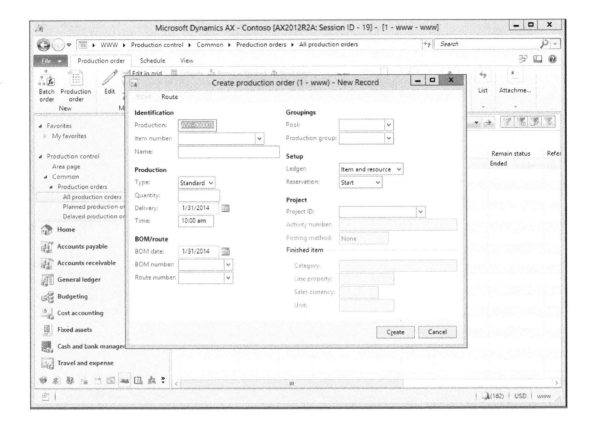

When the **Create Production Order** dialog box is displayed select the item that you want to create the job for from the **Item Number** dropdown list.

Creating Route Based Production Orders

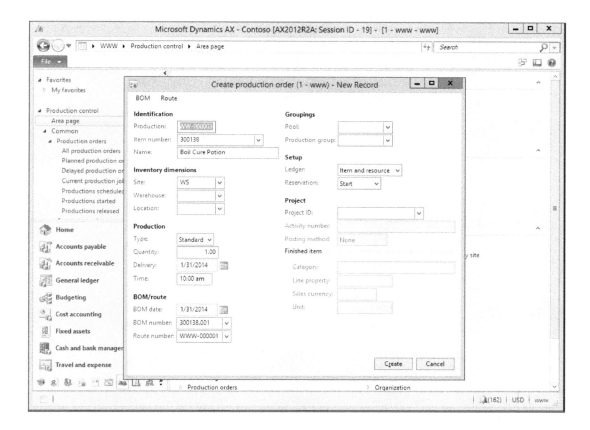

This should default in all of the information for the production job, including the active BOM and Route.

Creating Route Based Production Orders

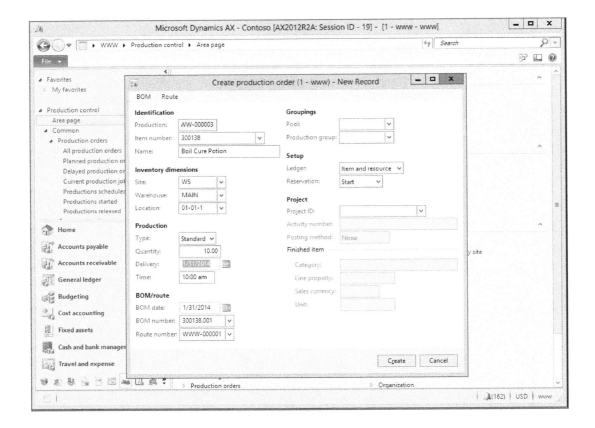

All you may need to do is update the **Quantity** and also may be update the **Warehouse** and output **Location.**

When you are ready to create the production order just click on the **Create** button.

Creating Route Based Production Orders

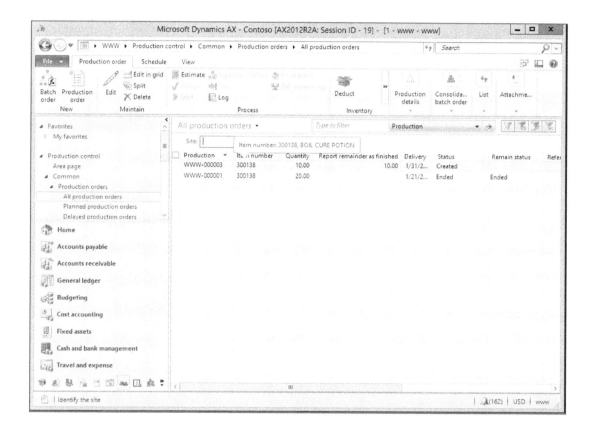

Now you will see that you have a new Production Order.

Creating Route Based Production Orders

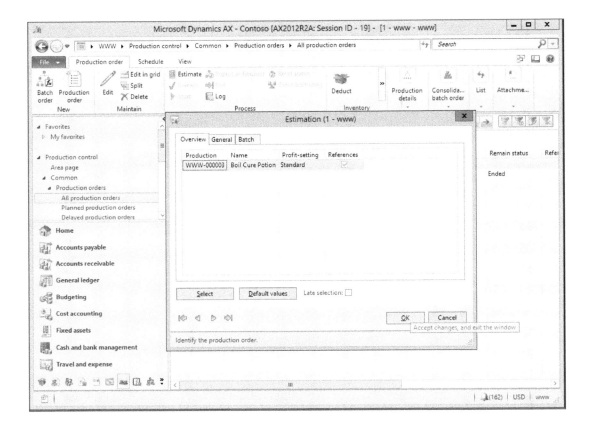

All of the same steps apply to this production order as the earlier one. If you want to release the production order to the shop floor and reserve the inventory, just click on the **Estimate** button within the **Process** group of the **Production Order** ribbon bar, select the production order and click on the **OK** button.

Creating Route Based Production Orders

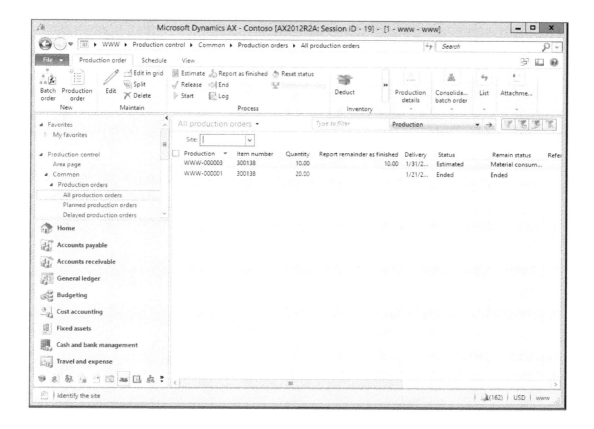

How simple is that?

Scheduling Job Operations

Now that our production jobs have **Route** information associated with them we can start getting clever and use the inbuilt scheduler within the Production area to graphically plan all of our production.

Scheduling Job Operations

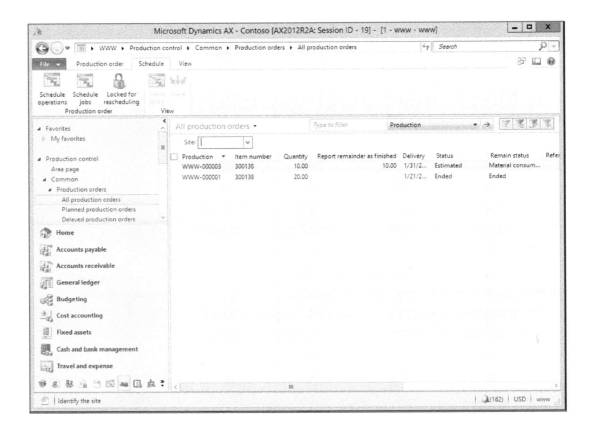

From within the **All Production Orders** list page, select the production job(s) that you want to schedule, and then click on the **Schedule Jobs** button within the **Production Order** group of the **Schedule** ribbon bar.

Note: if you remember back to the Route Operation line configuration step, there was an option on the resource management to select if the resource was to be used for Job, or Operation scheduling. In this spect, you can also click on the **Schedule Operations** button, and it will schedule all of the resources that you have marked for Operation Scheduling.

Scheduling Job Operations

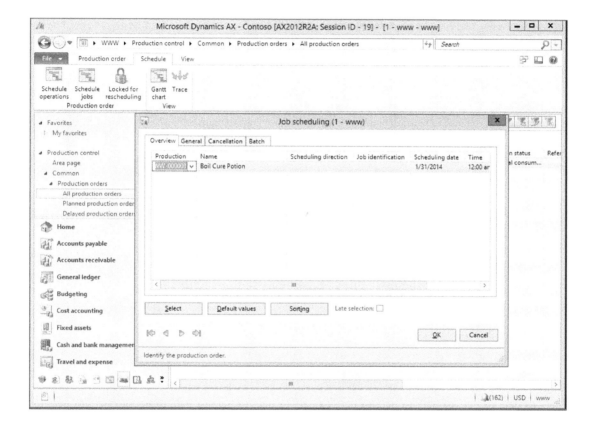

When the **Job Scheduling** dialog box is shown, just click the **OK** button to start he scheduling process.

Scheduling Job Operations

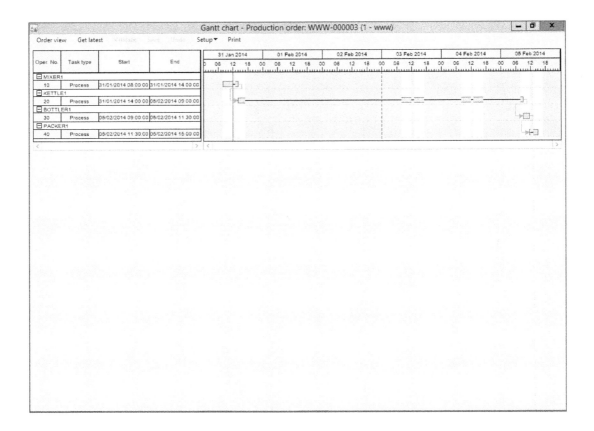

The Scheduling Gantt Chart should then be displayed with all of your resources listed, and also the jobs laid out in a time sequence.

You can move the operations around as you like which will update the production jobs with the new start and end times.

Starting Scheduled Production Jobs

Once you have scheduled your jobs, all you have to do to send them down to the shop floor is to start them. In the previous chapter we went through the Release step first and then started the job, but if you have your production parameters configured to allow bypassing that step, then you can just start them.

Starting Scheduled Production Jobs

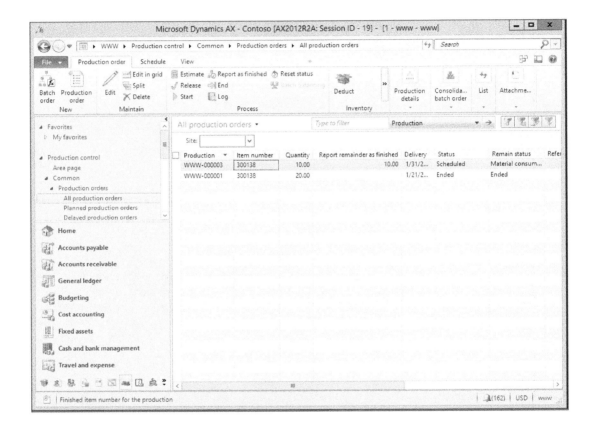

From within the **All Production Orders** list page, select the production job(s) that you want to start, and click the **Start** button within the **Process** group of the **Production Order** ribbon bar.

Starting Scheduled Production Jobs

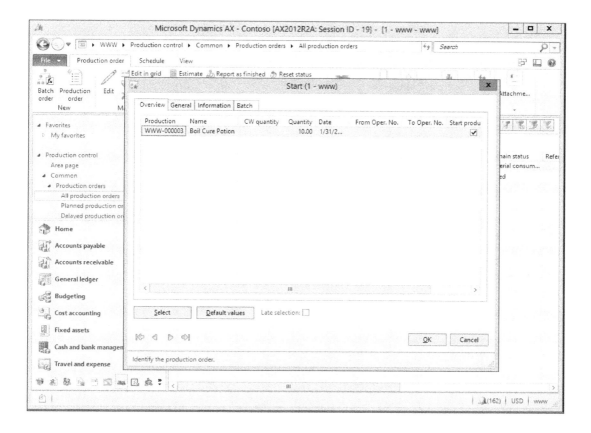

When the list of jobs are displayed within the **Start** dialog box, just click the **OK** button.

Starting Scheduled Production Jobs

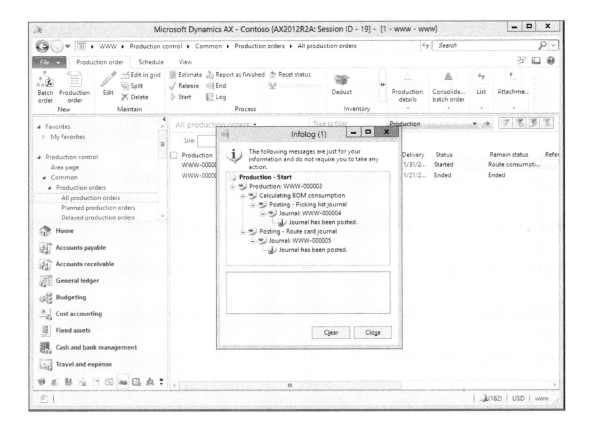

Now you should receive an Infolog that shows all of the activity that was performed as a result. Notice that in addition to the system creating the Picking journals, you also have a **Route Card Journal** that was created as well that will allow you to report time against the job and track the overhead costs of the operations.

Using The Job List To Update Production Jobs

If you want to view all of the production jobs that are running and also update their details, then you can do that through the **Edit Job List** function. This will allow you to see all of the production detail, move the operations to other resources, and also report time and material all through one simple view.

Using The Job List To Update Production Jobs

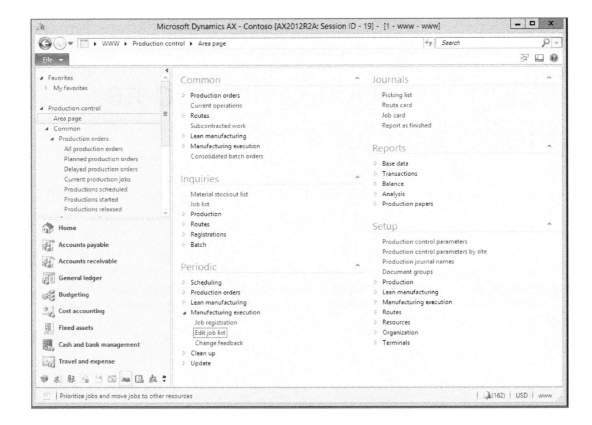

Click on the **Edit Job List** menu item within the **Manufacturing Execution** folder of the **Periodic** group of the **Production Control** area page.

Using The Job List To Update Production Jobs

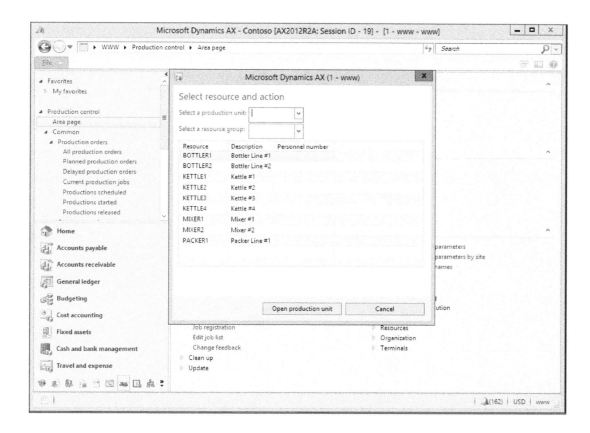

When the **Select Resource And Action** dialog box is displayed, you will see all of the **Resources** that you can view the details for.

Using The Job List To Update Production Jobs

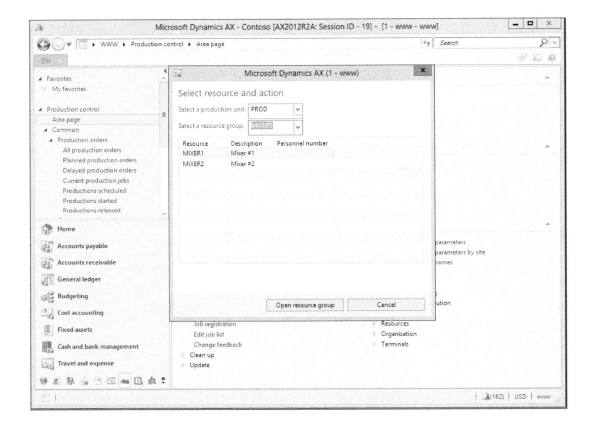

If you update the **Production Unit** and the **Resource Group** then you will see just the **Resources** within that area.

Using The Job List To Update Production Jobs

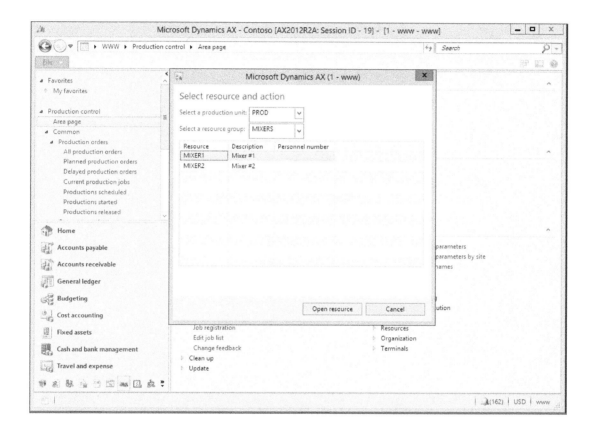

All you need to do is click on the **Resource** that you want to view the jobs for and click the **Open Resource** butoon.

Using The Job List To Update Production Jobs

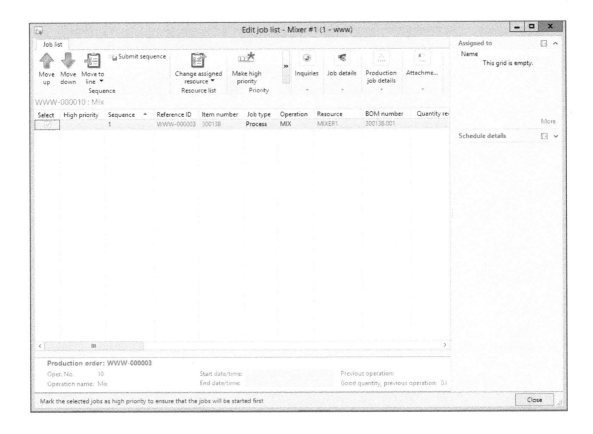

Now you will see the production job that is scheduled for the resource.

Using The Job List To Update Production Jobs

If you click on the **Change Assigned Resource** menu button within the **Resource List** group of the **Job List** ribbon bar, then a dropdown will be displayed that allows you to change your **Resource** associated with the operation.

Using The Job List To Update Production Jobs

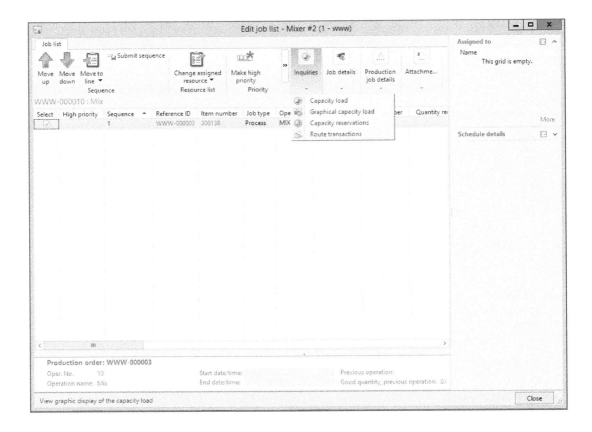

If you want to view how much capacity each of the resource groups have, then click on the **Graphical Capacity Load** button within the **Inquiries** group of the **Jobs List** ribbon bar.

Using The Job List To Update Production Jobs

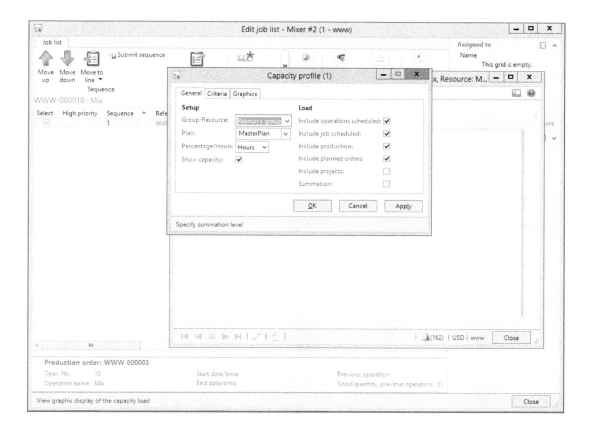

When the **Capacity Profile** dialog box is displayed, just click the **OK** button.

Using The Job List To Update Production Jobs

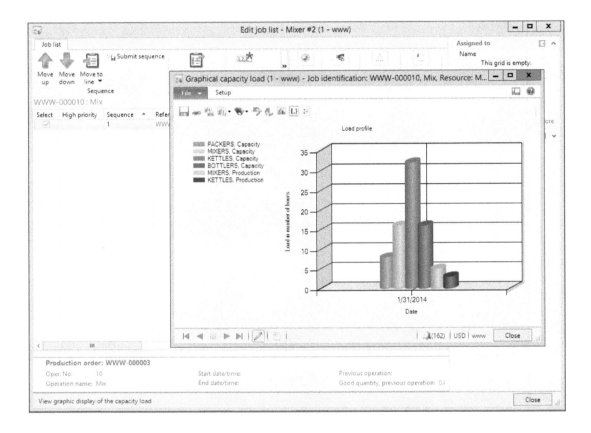

You should then be able to see the **Graphical Capacity Load** for all of the **Resource Groups**.

Using The Job List To Update Production Jobs

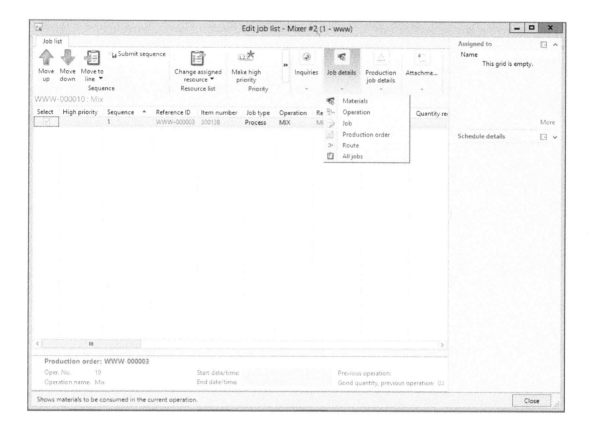

Also, if you want to see any of the job details then you can view those from here as well. To view all of the **Materials** associated with this job operation, click on the **Materials** button within the **Job Details** group of the **Job List** ribbon bar.

Using The Job List To Update Production Jobs

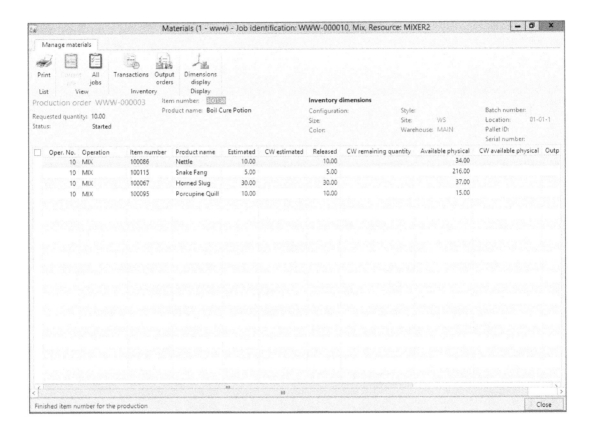

When the **Materials** form is displayed you will be able to see everything that you need to issue to the production operation.

Viewing All Job Operations

Another way that you can view all of the current operation is through the **Production Jobs** form. This allows you to see all of the operations at once, making it easier to track down operations that you may not know the resource that they are running on.

Viewing All Job Operations

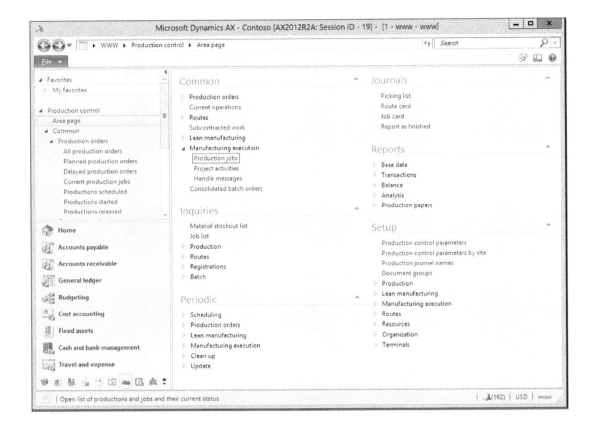

To view all the operations, click on the **Production Jobs** menu item within the **Manufacturing Execution** folder of the **Common** group of the **Production Control** area page.

Viewing All Job Operations

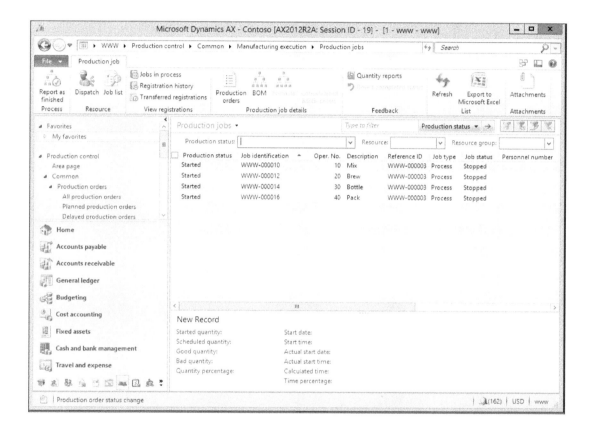

When the **Production Jobs** list page is displayed you will see all of the operations that are being processed.

It's like a well oiled machine.

CONFIGURING JOB REGISTRATION

Dynamics AX has a nifty feature built into it that allows all of the production transactions to be performed through **Registration Terminals**. These are not your typical screen though because they have been designed to be ran through a shared Kiosk and allow workers to clock in, view their jobs that they have been assigned, report production, and then clock out, all through a touch screen enabled form.

This is a great alternative view for production, especially if you don't want to give all of the workers PC's or have them access the more detailed screens in Dynamics AX. All you need to do is a little configuration and you are up and running.

Configuring Indirect Activity Categories

Before we can use the **Registration Terminals** though there is a little bit of setup that is required. The first step is to configure some **Indirect Activity Category** codes. These will be used to track all of the activities that you will be performing within the Job Registration.

Configuring Indirect Activity Categories

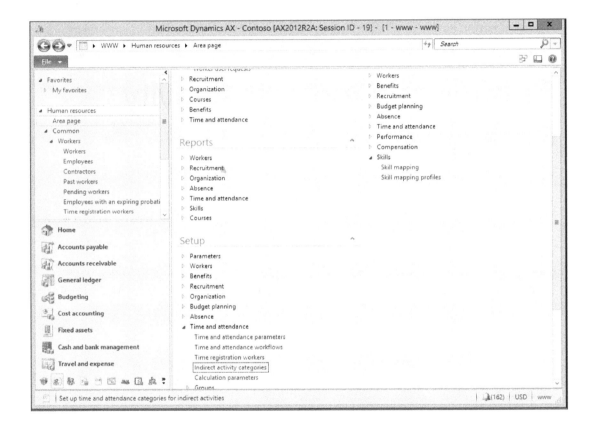

To set these up, click on the **Indirect Activity Categories** menu item within the **Time and Attendance** folder of the **Setup** group within the **Human Resources** area page.

Configuring Indirect Activity Categories

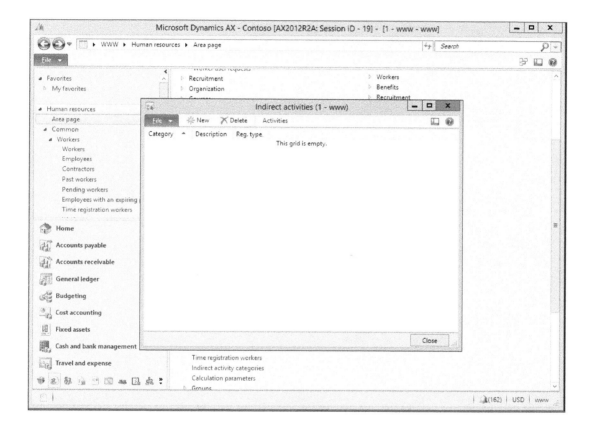

When the **Indirect Activities** maintenance form is displayed, click on the **New** button in the menu bar to add a new record.

Configuring Indirect Activity Categories

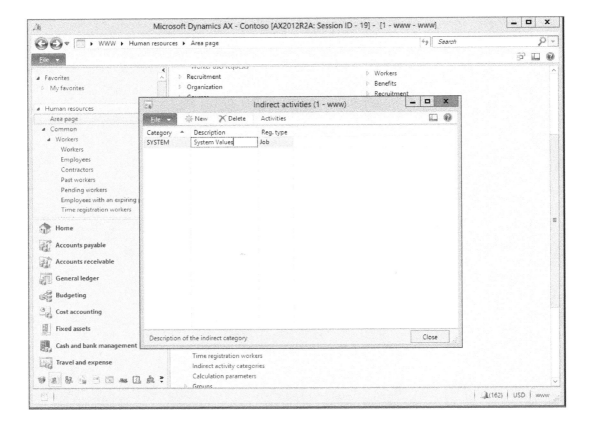

Set the **Category** code to **SYSTEM**, add a **Description**.

Make sure that the **Reg Type** is **Job**, and then click on the **Activities** button within the menu bar.

Configuring Indirect Activity Categories

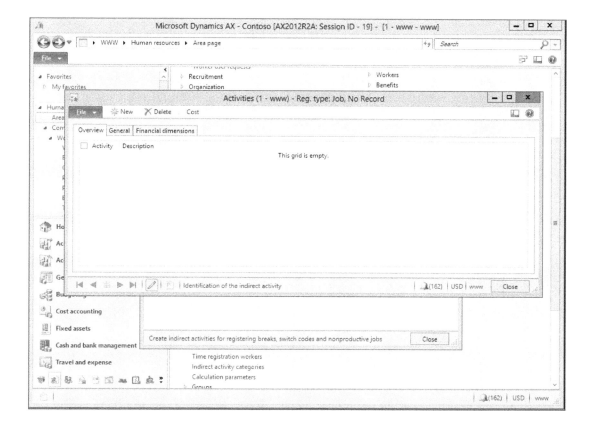

When the **Activities** maintenance form is displayed, we can start adding in all of the different activities that we want to track within the Job Registration.

To start doing that, click on the **New** button in the menu bar.

Configuring Indirect Activity Categories

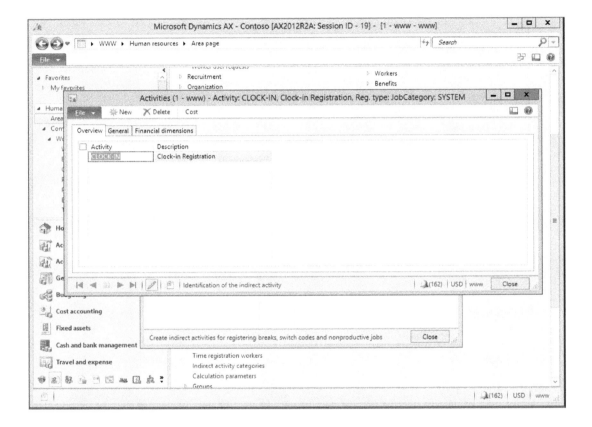

Set the first **Activity** code to **CLOCK-IN** and add a description.

Configuring Indirect Activity Categories

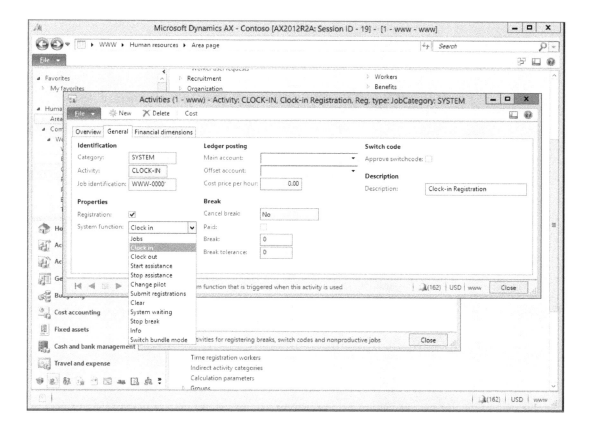

Then switch to the **General** tab, and within the **Properties** group, click on the **System Function** drop down, and select the **Clock-In** value.

Configuring Indirect Activity Categories

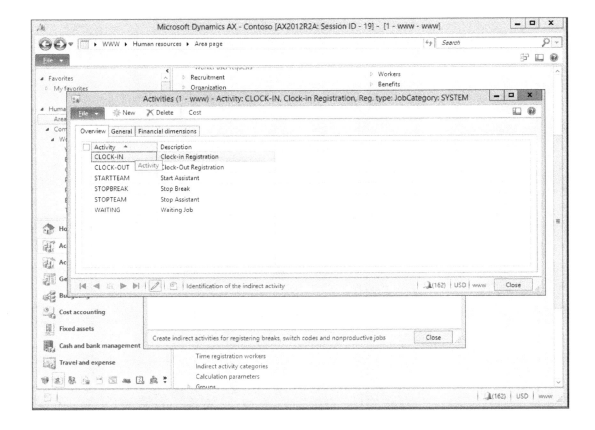

Repeat the process for **CLOCK-OUT**, **STARTTAM**, **STOPBREAK**, **STOPTEAM**, and **WAITING**.

Activating Employees for Job Registration

Now we need to configure the Worker records so that they are able to use the **Registration Terminals**.

Activating Employees for Job Registration

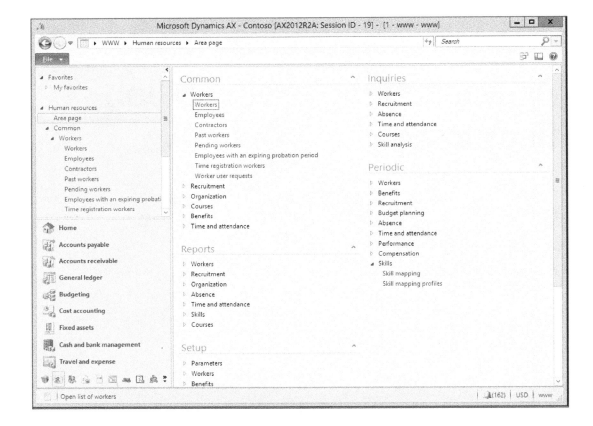

To do this, click on the **Workers** menu item within the **Workers** folder of the **Common** group of the **Human Resources** area page.

Activating Employees for Job Registration

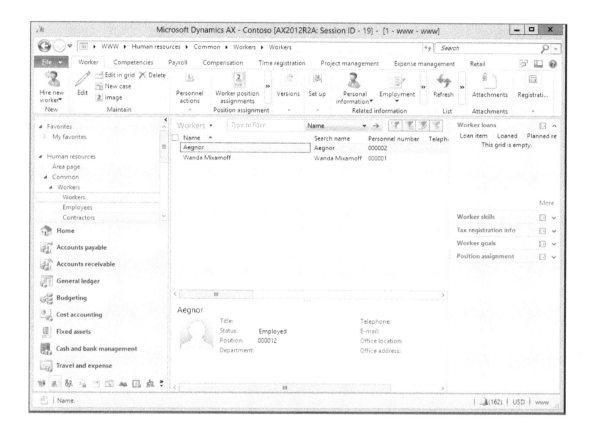

When the **Workers** list page is displayed, select the **Worker** record that you want to enable on the **Registration Terminals** and click on the **Edit** button within the **Maintain** group of the **Worker** ribbon bar to open up the **Workes** detail page.

Activating Employees for Job Registration

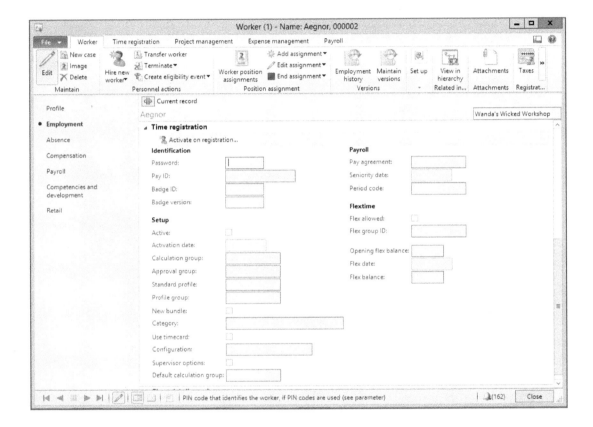

When the **Worker** detail form is displayed, switch to the **Employment** page, and click on the **Activate on Registration** menu button within the **Time Registration** tab.

Activating Employees for Job Registration

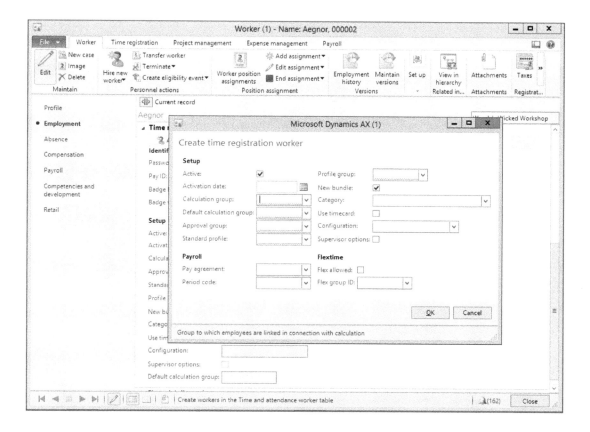

When the **Create Time Registration Worker** dialog box is displayed, right-mouse-click on the **Calculation Group** field and select the **View Details** option.

Activating Employees for Job Registration

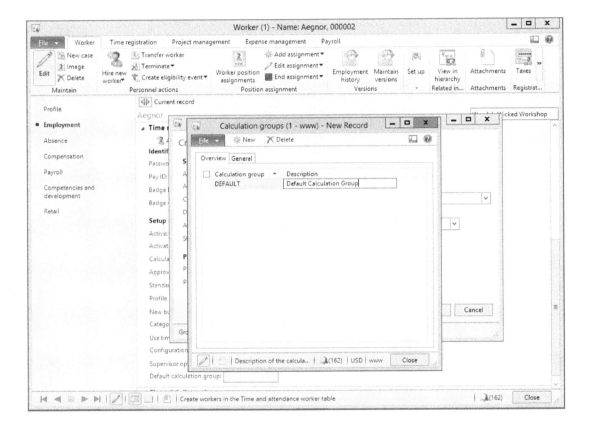

When the **Calculation Groups** maintenance form is displayed, click on the **New** button in the menu bar to create a new record and assign it a **Calculation Group** code and a **Description**. Then click on the **Close** button to exit from the form.

Activating Employees for Job Registration

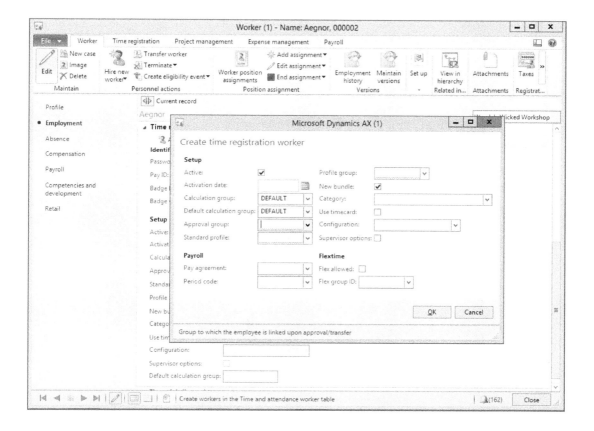

Now you can use that **Calculation Group** code within the **Calculation Group**, and **Default Calculation Group** fields.

Next right-mouse-click on the **Approval Group** field and select the **View Details** option.

Activating Employees for Job Registration

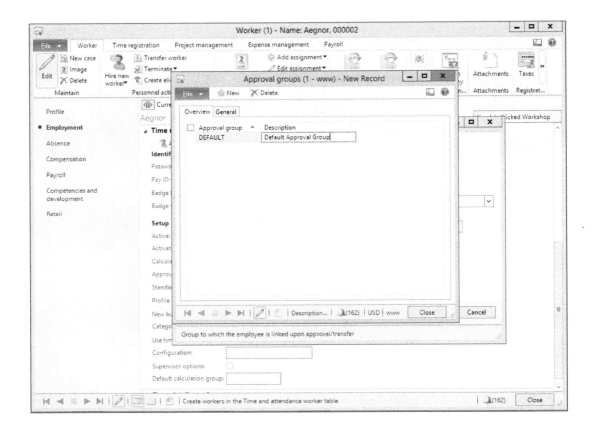

When the **Approval Groups** maintenance form is displayed, click on the **New** button in the menu bar to create a new record and assign it a **Approval Group** code and a **Description**. Then click on the **Close** button to exit from the form.

Activating Employees for Job Registration

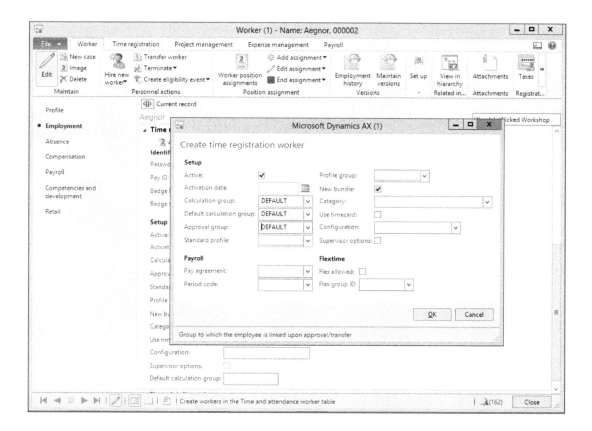

Then assign the **Approval Group** code to the **Approval Group** field.

Right-mouse-click again on the **Standard Profile** field and select the **View Details** option.

Activating Employees for Job Registration

When the **Profiles** maintenance form is displayed, click on the **New** button to create a new record.

Activating Employees for Job Registration

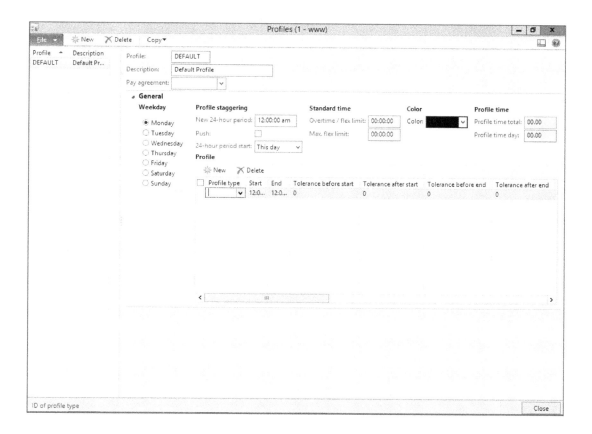

Assign your new record a **Profile** code, and a **Description**.

Then click the **New** button at the top of the **Profile** list within the **General** tab to create a new record.

Right-mouse-click again on the **Profile Type** field and select the **View Details** option.

Activating Employees for Job Registration

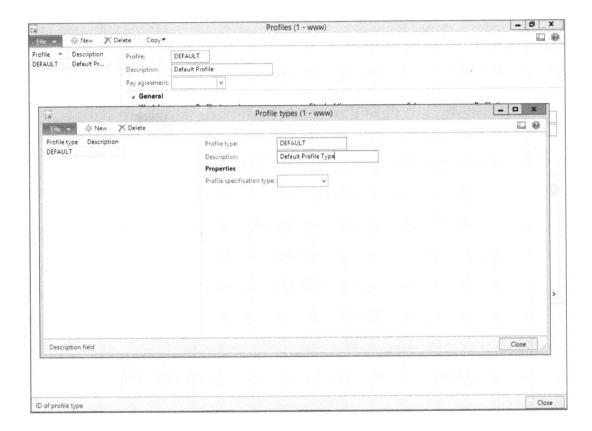

When the **Profile Types** maintenance form is displayed, click on the **New** button in the menu bar to create a new record and assign the record a **Profile Type** code and **Description**. Then click on the **Close** button to exit from the form.

Activating Employees for Job Registration

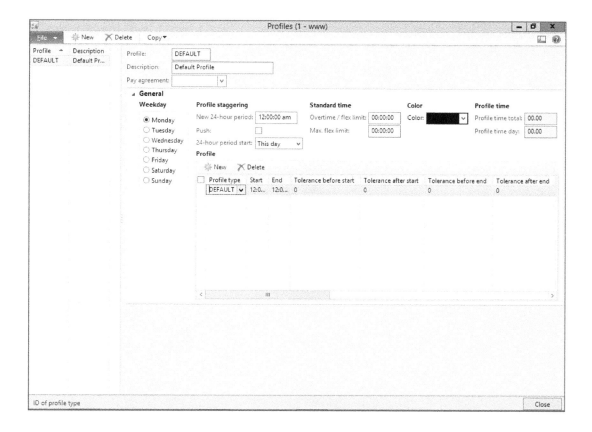

When you return to the **Profiles** maintenance form, set the **Profile Type** field to be your new **Profile Type** code that you just created,

Activating Employees for Job Registration

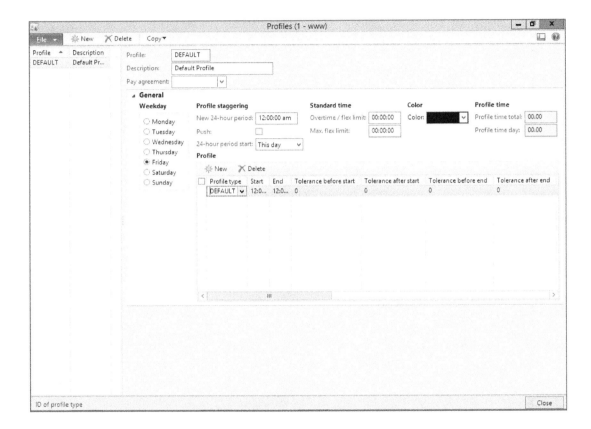

Repeat the process (minus the **Profile** Type creation) For each of the **Weekdays** that you want to allow the user to use the Job Registration forms.

When you are done, you can click on the Close button to exit the form.

Note: if you have different shifts, or want to create different profiles for weekdays and weekends then you can create more profiles.

Activating Employees for Job Registration

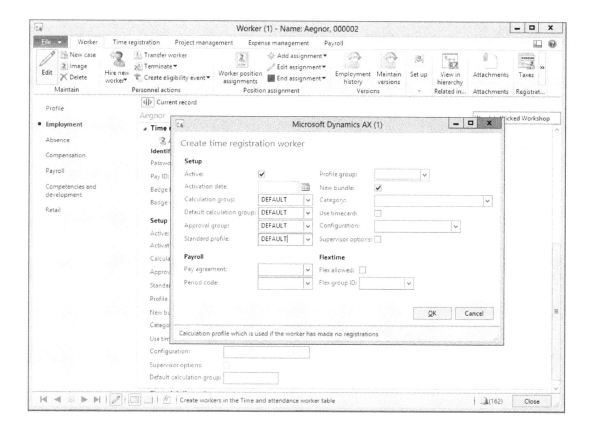

Now assign the **Profile** code that you just created to the **Standard Profile** field.

Right-mouse-click again on the **Profile Group** field and select the **View Details** option.

Activating Employees for Job Registration

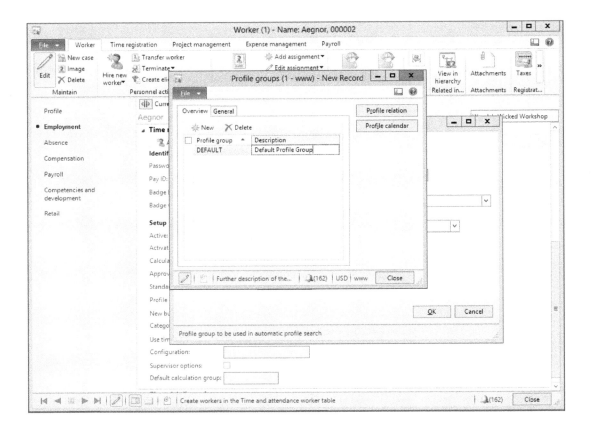

When the **Profile Groups** maintenance form is displayed, click on the **New** button in the menu bar to create a new record and assign it a **Profile Group** code and a **Description**.

Click on the **Profile Relation** button to the right of the form.

Activating Employees for Job Registration

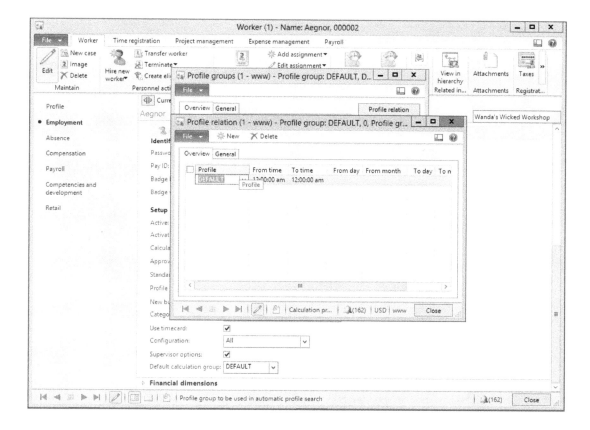

When the **Profile Relation** maintenance form is displayed, click on the **New** button to create a new record and then select the default **Profile** code that you want to link to the **Profile** group.

Now click on the **Close** button to exit from the forms.

Activating Employees for Job Registration

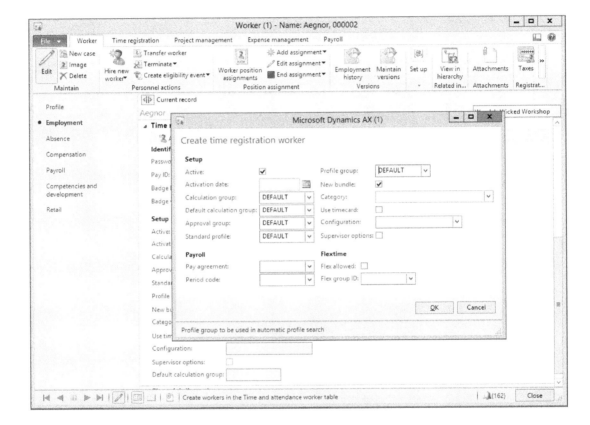

Assign the **Profile Group** code that you just created to the **Profile Group** field.

Now that all of the configuration and codes has been completed, click on the **OK** button.

Activating Employees for Job Registration

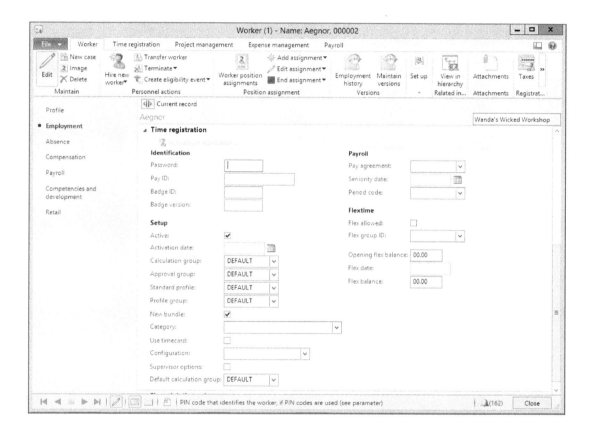

When you return to the **Worker** form, you will see that all of the codes have been assigned, and also the work should have the **Active** flag set against them.

Activating Employees for Job Registration

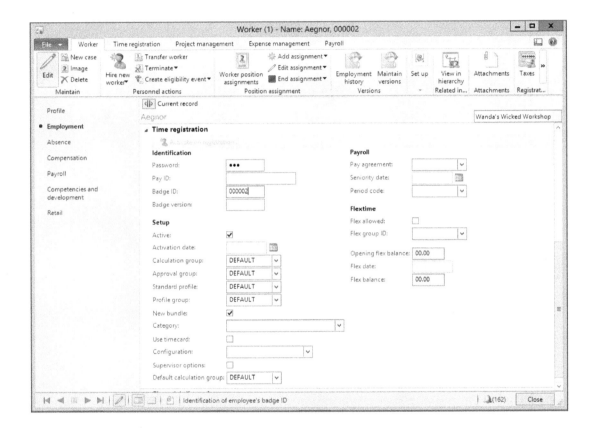

Now you can assign the user a **Password** and also a **Badge ID** if you want to use badge scanning in lieu of entering a password.

Activating Employees for Job Registration

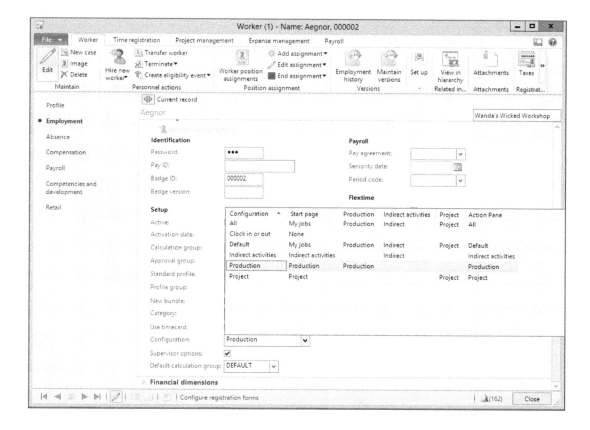

From the **Configuration** dropdown, select the type of Registration Form that you want to have the user use by default – in this case we will use the **Production** config.

Activating Employees for Job Registration

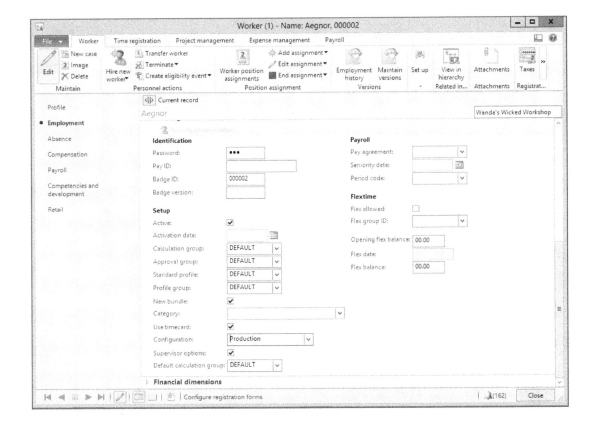

And finally, if you want the time to be reported for timecard and payroll tracking then check the **Use Timecard** flag.

Now you can click the **Close** button and exit from the form.

Accessing Job Registration Terminals

Now that you have your Worker configured for the Registration forms, you can let them log in and start working.

Accessing Job Registration Terminals

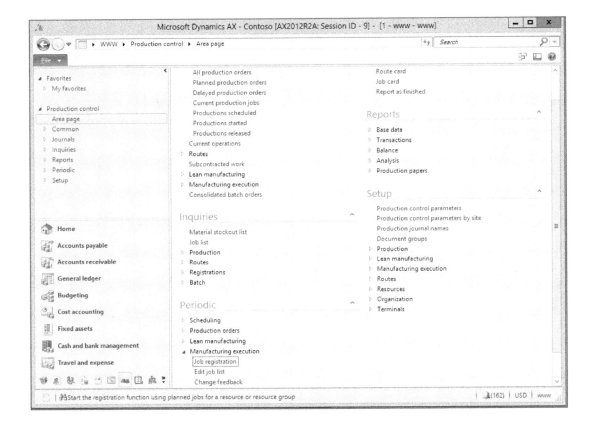

To do this, click on the **Job Registration** menu item within the **Manufacturing Execution folder of the** Periodic **group within the** Production Control **area page.**

Accessing Job Registration Terminals

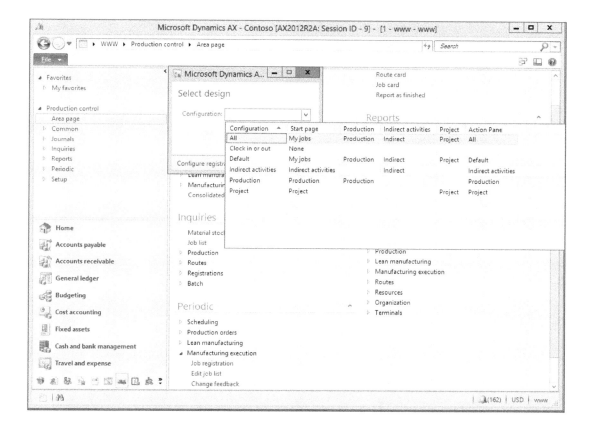

If this is the first time that you have logged in, then it will ask you for the design that you want to use for your Registration Screen.

Accessing Job Registration Terminals

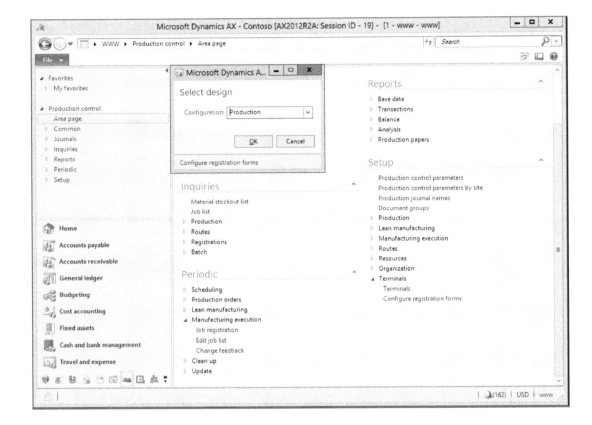

Select the **Production Configuration** and then click on the **OK** button.

Accessing Job Registration Terminals

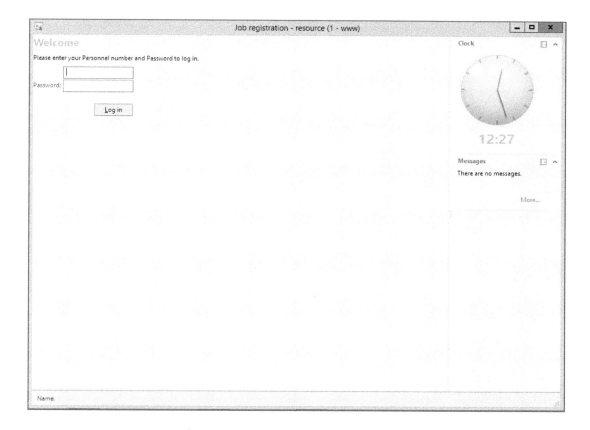

When the **Job Registration** form is displayed, it will be in Clock-In mode ready for you to start performing tasks.

Using The Registration Terminals To Track Attendance

One of the ways that the managers are able to use the Registration Terminals is to track the workers, and see who has clocked in and started work.

Using The Registration Terminals To Track Attendance

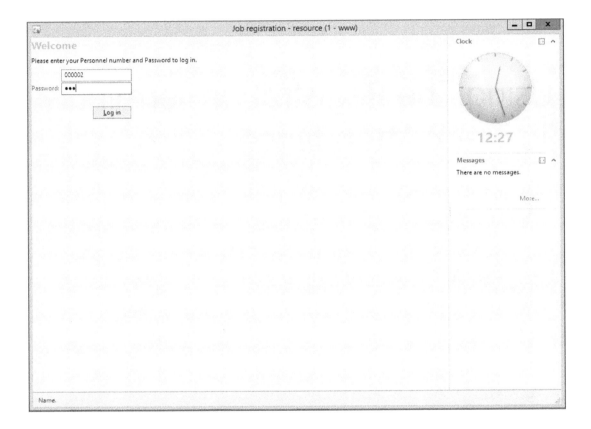

All you need to do is enter in the **Worker ID** and **Password**, and then click on the **Log in** button.

Using The Registration Terminals To Track Attendance

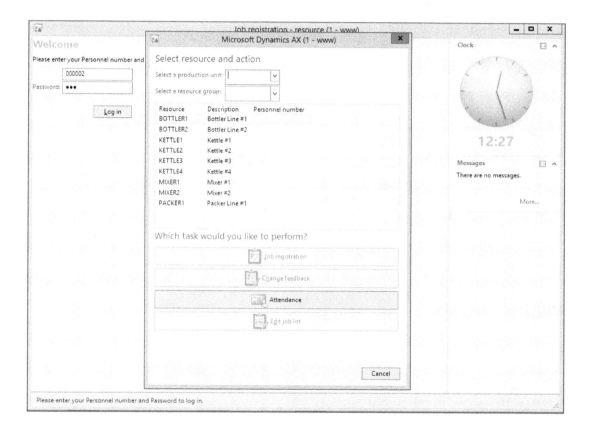

You will then be asked which resource are you wanting to clock into, and what actions are you performing.

Using The Registration Terminals To Track Attendance

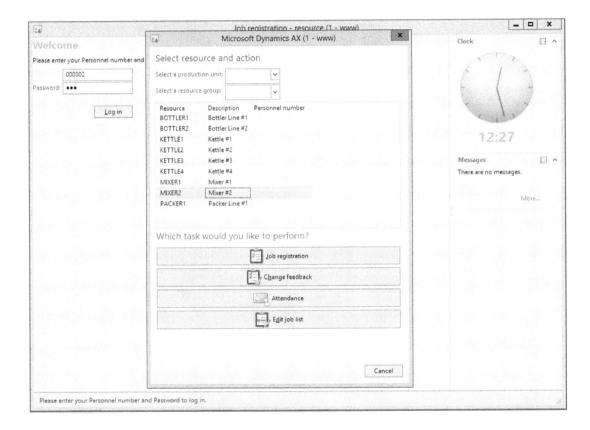

From here you can click on the **Attendance** button will still be enabled at the bottom.

Note: If you do select the **Resource** from the Resource list then more options will be enabled.

Using The Registration Terminals To Track Attendance

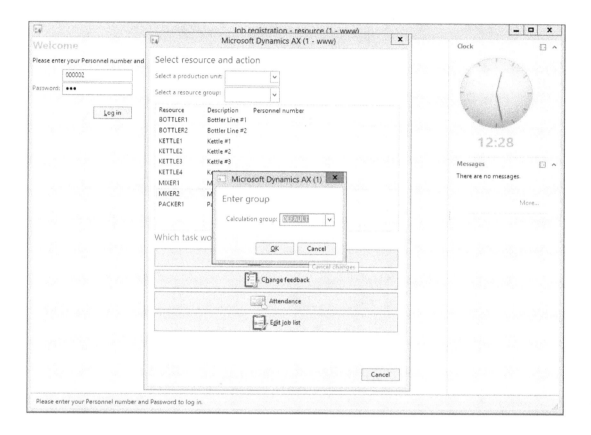

When the **Enter Group** dialog box is displayed, select the **Calculation Group** from the drop down and then click the **OK** button.

Using The Registration Terminals To Track Attendance

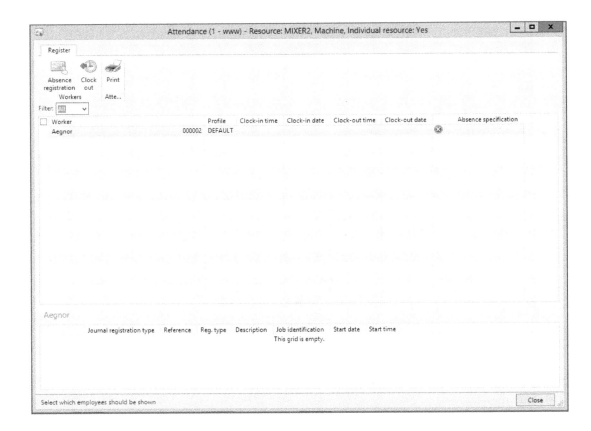

Now you will be able to see all of your employees and if they are working or not.

Converting Registration Terminals To Touchscreen

If you are using the **Registration** forms in more of a kiosk mode, then you may want to make a small tweak to the format and covert them to touchscreen mode. This will make the buttons just a little bigger, and also change the input method that you can use from just the keyboard to an on-screen touchpad.

Converting Registration Terminals To Touchscreen

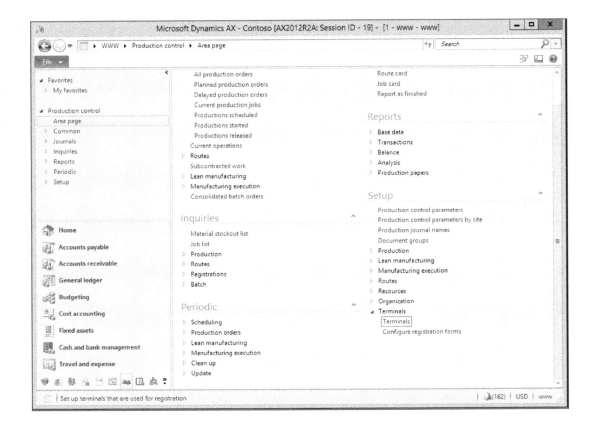

To do this for an existing terminal, click on the **Terminals** menu item within the **Terminals** folder of the **Setup** group within the **Production Control** area page.

Converting Registration Terminals To Touchscreen

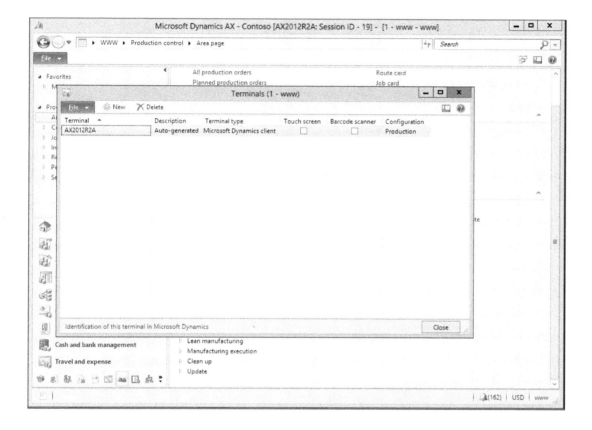

When the **Terminals** maintenance form is displayed, you will see all of the active terminals that are being used.

Converting Registration Terminals To Touchscreen

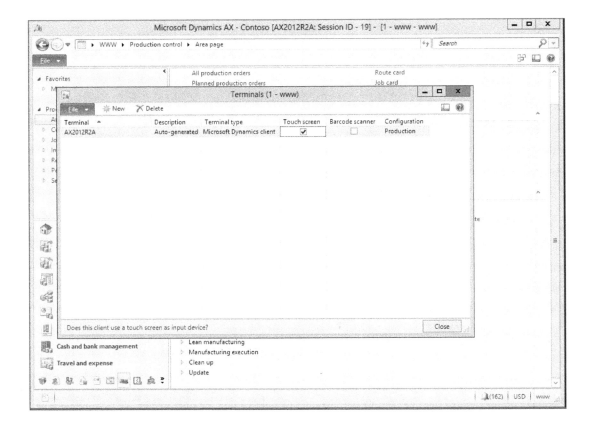

Just check the **Touchscreen** flag on the terminal and then click the **Close** button.

Converting Registration Terminals To Touchscreen

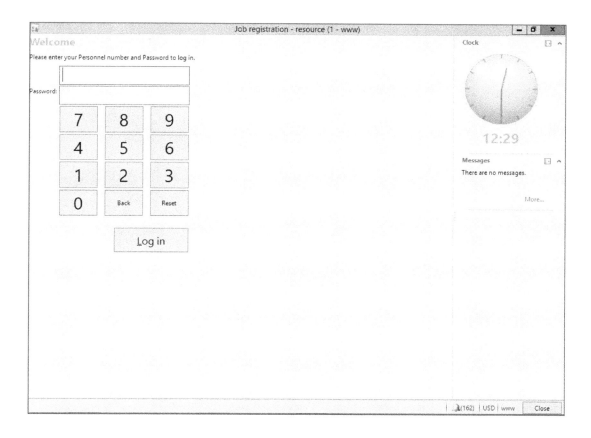

Now when you use the **Registration** form you will notice that it has changed a little.

Converting Registration Terminals To Touchscreen

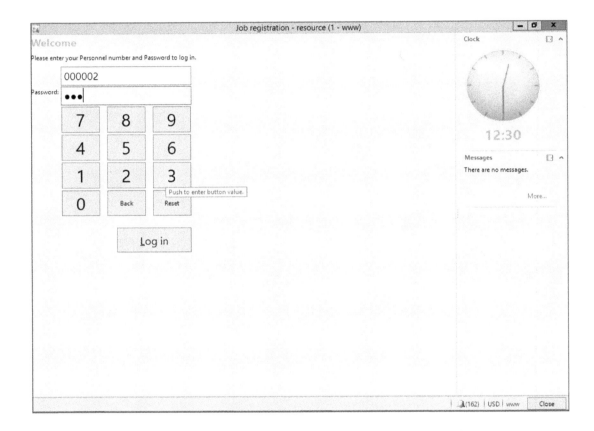

Now you can enter in your ID and also your password through the on screen keypad.

Converting Registration Terminals To Touchscreen

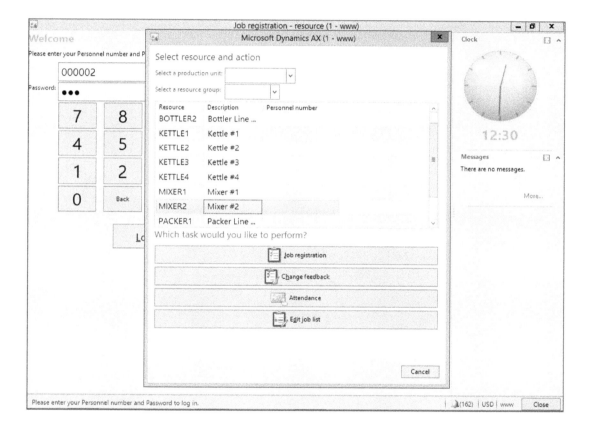

And when you see the **Select Resource and Action** dialog box, you will notice that it is a little larger to accommodate the use of fingers.

How cool is that!

Accessing Job Details Through The Registration Terminals

Once you have the Registration Terminals configured the way that you like them you can start using them to view all of your Production information.

Accessing Job Details Through The Registration Terminals

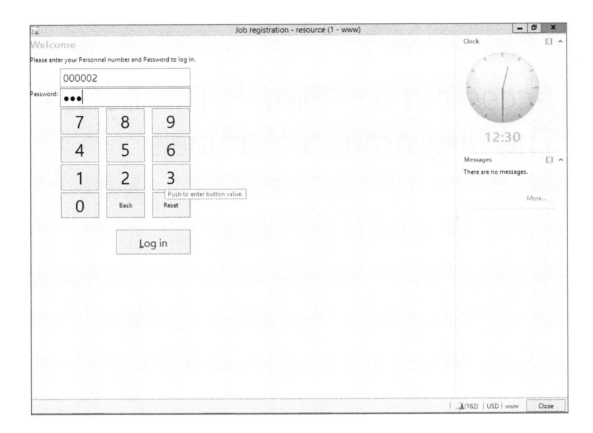

Open up the **Job Registration** terminal; and enter in your ID and also your password through the on screen keypad.

Accessing Job Details Through The Registration Terminals

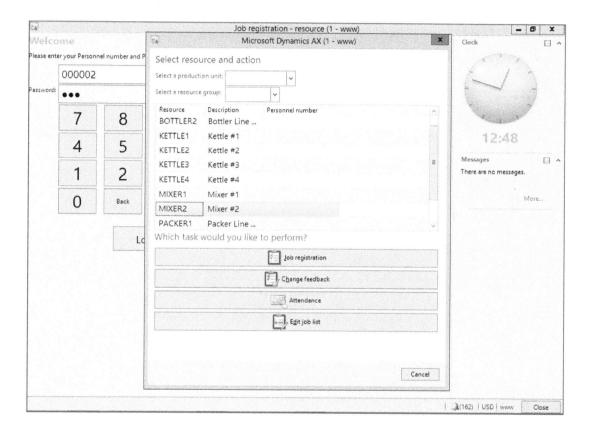

When the **Select Resource And Action** dialog box is displayed, select the **Resource** that you want to start working on and then click on the **Job Registration** button.

Accessing Job Details Through The Registration Terminals

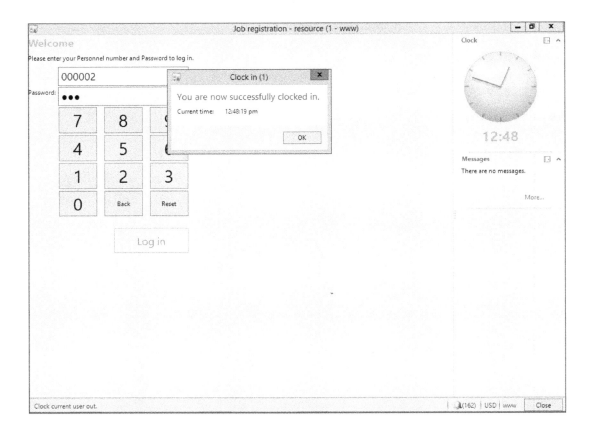

Since we have timecard registration turned on then Dynamics AX will automatically clock the user in.

Accessing Job Details Through The Registration Terminals

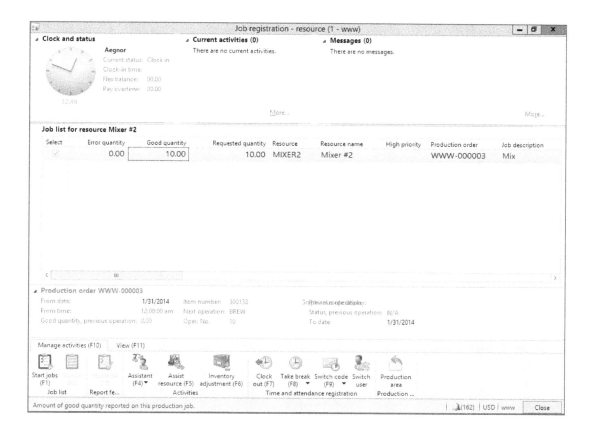

And then through the **Job Registration** form you can see all of the jobs that are currently assigned to the work center resource.

Starting Production Jobs Via The Registration Terminals

One of the major benefits of the Registration Terminals are that the users are able to perform all of the production activities directly from these touchscreens. And the first place to start is to start the job so that you can record the actual execution times.

Starting Production Jobs Via The Registration Terminals

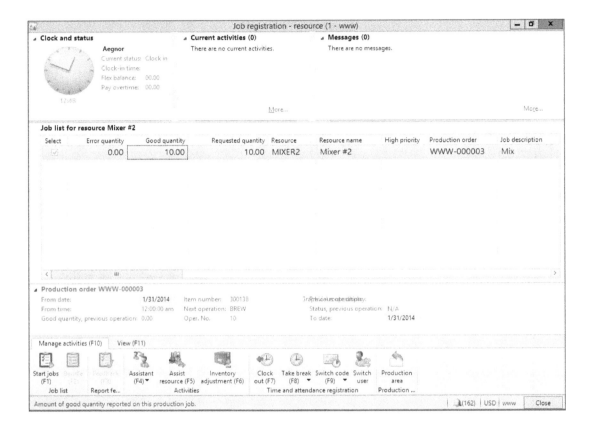

To do this, all you need to do is open up the Registration Terminal in Job Registration mode and select the job that you want to start working on and then click on the **Start Jobs** button within the **Jobs List** group of the **Manage Activities** ribbon bar.

Starting Production Jobs Via The Registration Terminals

After clicking on the button, the terminal will confirm that you have started the job, and you can just click on the **OK** button to exit out.

Reporting Job Output Via The Registration Terminals

Another task that you can perform through the Registration Terminals is the reporting of output product from the job operation.

Reporting Job Output Via The Registration Terminals

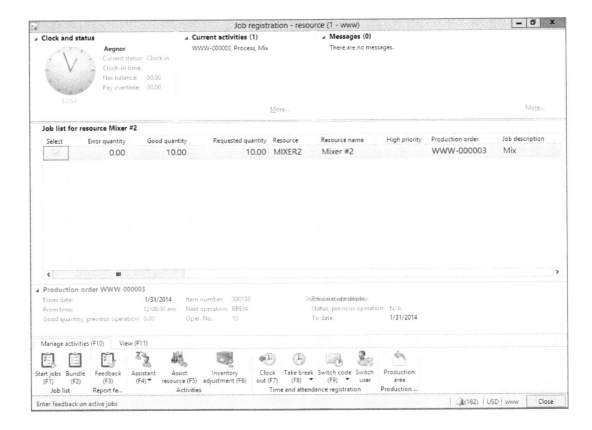

To do this, all you need to do is open up the Registration Terminal in Job Registration mode and select the job that you want to start working on and then click on the **Feedback** button within the **Jobs List** group of the **Manage Activities** ribbon bar.

Reporting Job Output Via The Registration Terminals

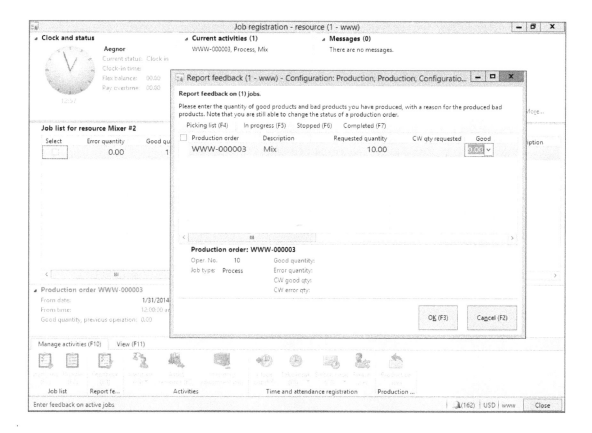

When the **Report Feedback** maintenance form is displayed, select the output line that you want to report out update the **Good** quantity value, and then click on the **OK** button.

Reporting Job Output Via The Registration Terminals

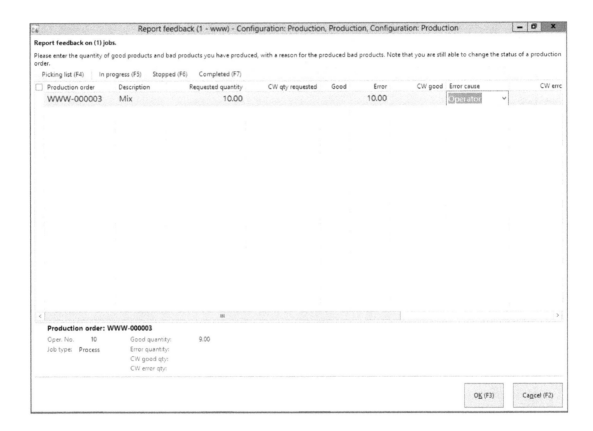

If you want to report error quantities then you can enter the quantity within the **Error** field and then select an **Error Cause** and then click the **OK** button.

Reporting Job Output Via The Registration Terminals

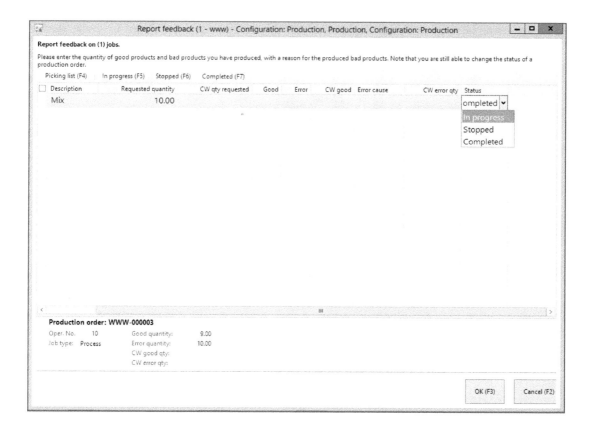

If you want to update the status of the resource then you can also update the **Status** field and then click the **OK** button.

Reporting Job Output Via The Registration Terminals

Once you have finished reporting your **Feedback** then the job will be removed from the operations for the Resource and you can move on to the next item in the list.

Switching Resource Within Job Registration

If you have workers that can work on multiple resources at once then they can switch from their current machine to another directly form within the **Job Registration** as well.

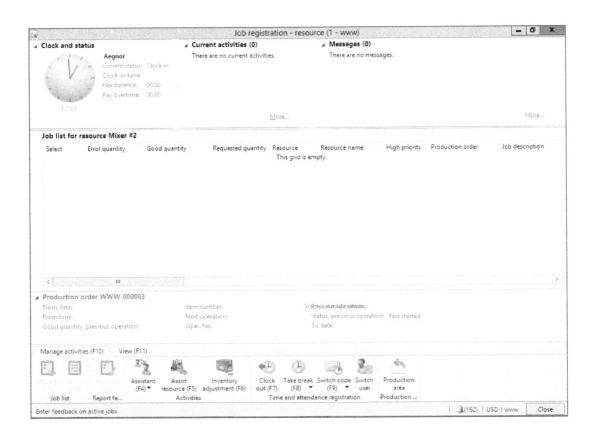

To do this, all you need to do is open up the Registration Terminal in Job Registration mode and select the job that you want to start working on and then click on the **Assist Resource** button within the **Activities** group of the **Manage Activities** ribbon bar.

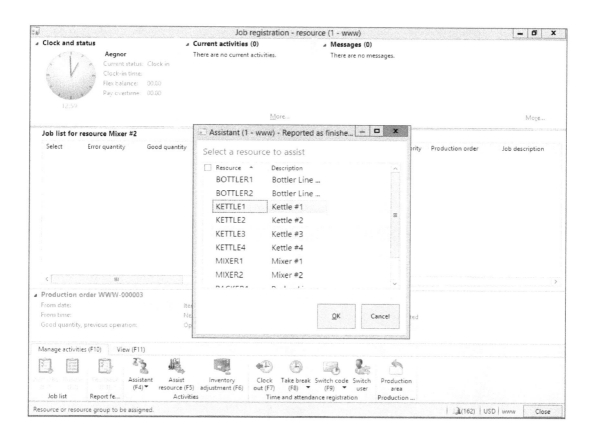

When the **Assist** dialog box is displayed, the user is able to select another resource and then click on the **OK** button.

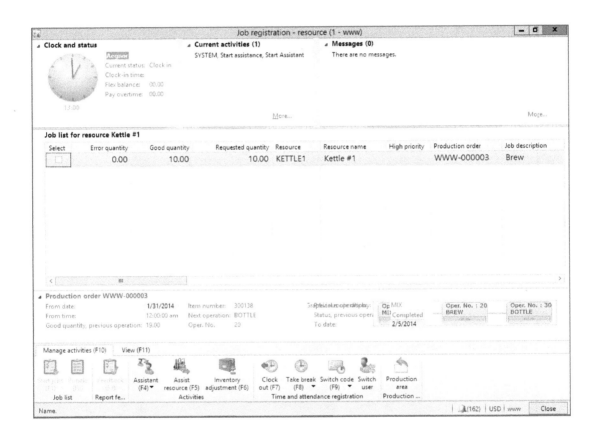

That will take them to the current jobs that are running on that resource and start reporting feedback there as well.

How easy is that!

Clocking Out Of Job Registration

Once the users have completes all of their tasks they can **Clock Out** directly from the **Job Registration** form as well.

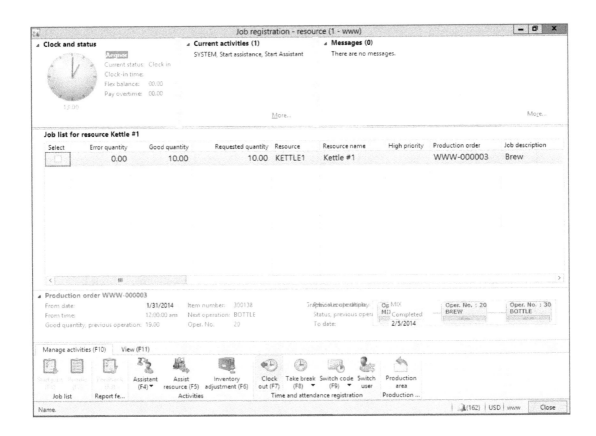

To do this click on the **Clock Out** button within the **Time and Attendance Registration** group of the **Manage Activities** ribbon bar.

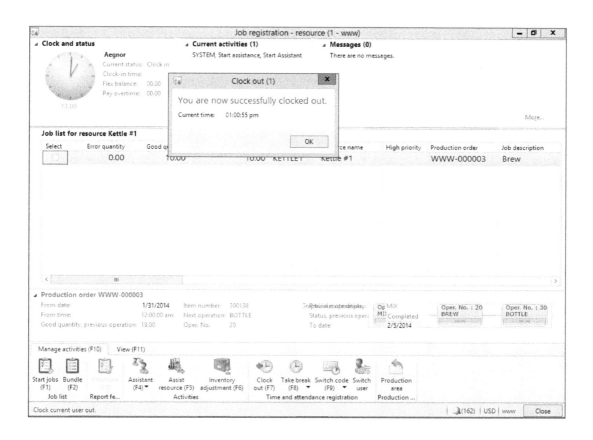

The **Registration Terminal** will then clock the worker out and report the time that has been spent on the resource.

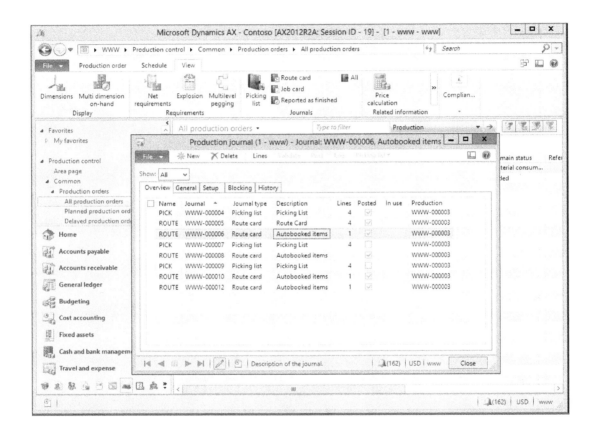

If you then look at the **Production Journal** for the job, then you will see that the **Route Card** has auto reported time associated with it where you can see all of the actual time that has been posted from the Job Registration Screens.

CONFIGURING WORK INSTRUCTIONS

Once you have configured all of the BOM's and Routes and are tracking the actual execution through the standard screens or through the **Registration Terminals** you can start working on ensuring that everything is done correctly. One way that you can do that is by configuring your **Work Instructions** so that they automatically show up ducting the production stages, and also requiring the users to review the documentation before they start working on the jobs.

Luckily this process is not hard to configure.

Creating A Work Instruction Document Type

In order to attach our **Work Instructions** to our production jobs, then we need to attach them as a **Document Attachment**. We can use any of the default document types if we like, although it may be a good idea to create a new **Document Type** that we can use to identify all of our Work Instructions.

Creating A Work Instruction Document Type

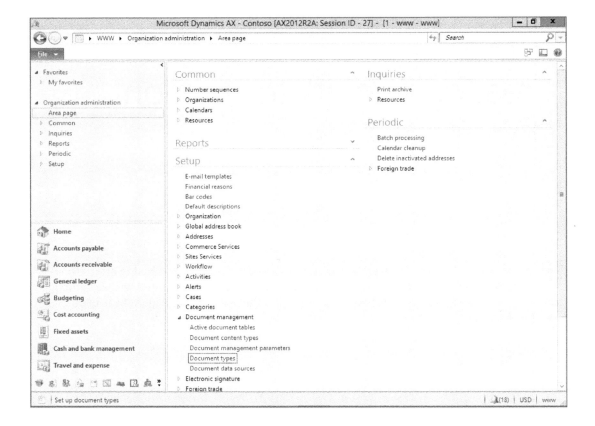

To do this, click on the **Document Types** menu item within the **Document Management** folder of the **Setup** group within the **Organization Administration** area page.

Creating A Work Instruction Document Type

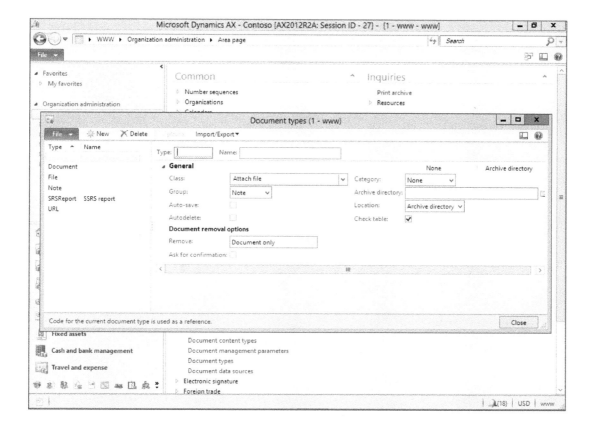

When the **Document Types** maintenance form is displayed, click on the **New** button in the menu bar to create a new record.

Creating A Work Instruction Document Type

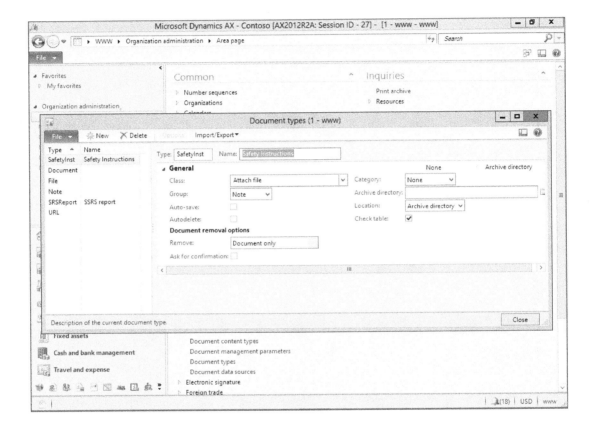

Assign your new record a Document **Type** code and a **Description.**

Creating A Work Instruction Document Type

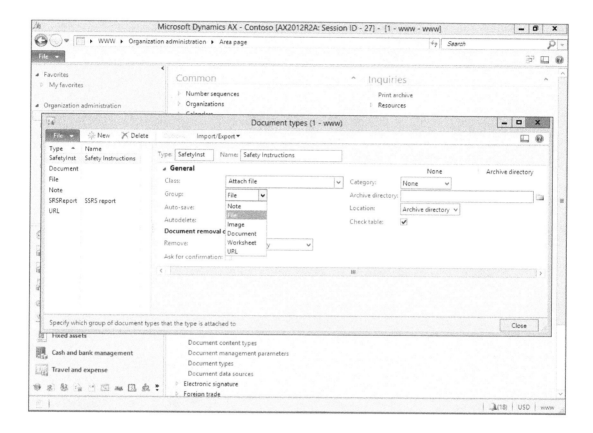

Set the Document **Group** code to be **File**.

Creating A Work Instruction Document Type

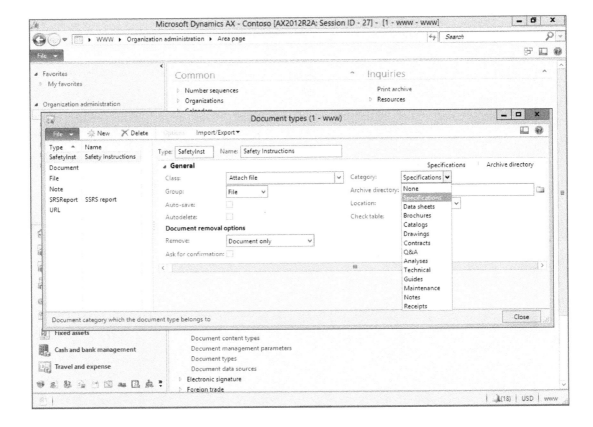

If you want you can assign the **Document Type** a **Category** to further segregate the documents.

Creating A Work Instruction Document Type

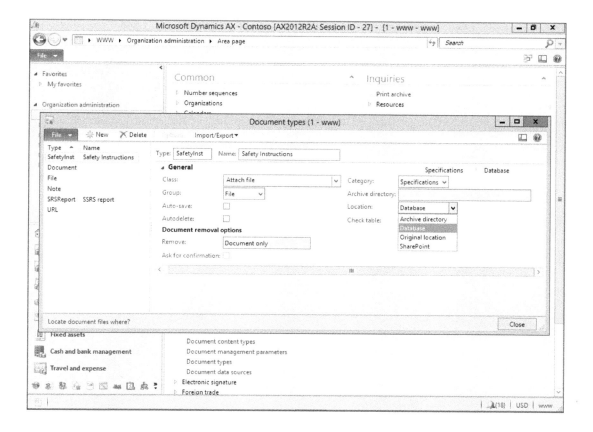

And then choose where you want to put the documents by select the **Location** from the dropdown list. In this case we will store all of our documents within the **Database**.

Creating A Work Instruction Document Type

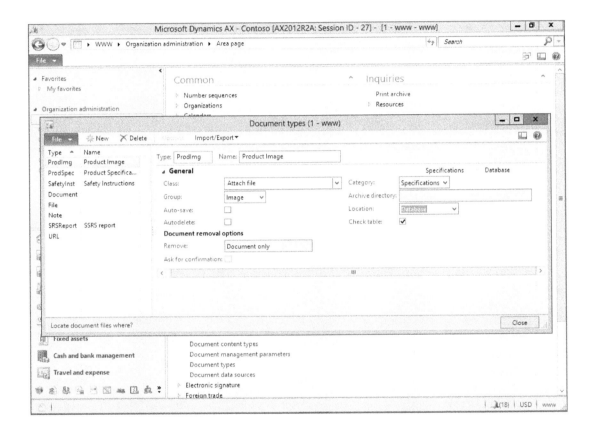

You can continue adding more **Document Types** for different types of work instruction documents.

When you are done, just click the **Close** button to exit from the form.

Creating Work Instruction Document Groups

Now that you have the **Document Types** created for your work instructions, you need to configure them to be used within production. In order to do that you need to configure the **Document Groups** to include them.

Creating Work Instruction Document Groups

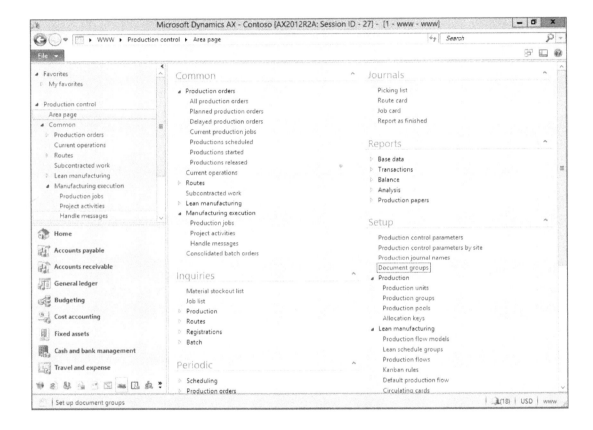

To do this, click on the **Document Groups** menu item within the **Setup** group of the **Production Control** area page.

Creating Work Instruction Document Groups

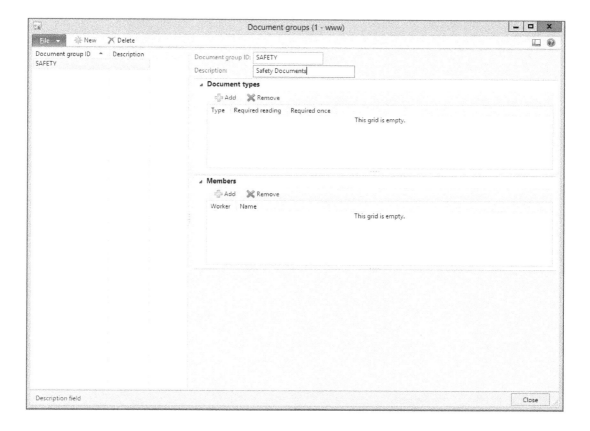

When the **Document Groups** maintenance form is displayed, click on the **New** button in the menu bar to create a new record and then adding your record a **Document Group ID** code, and a **Description**.

Creating Work Instruction Document Groups

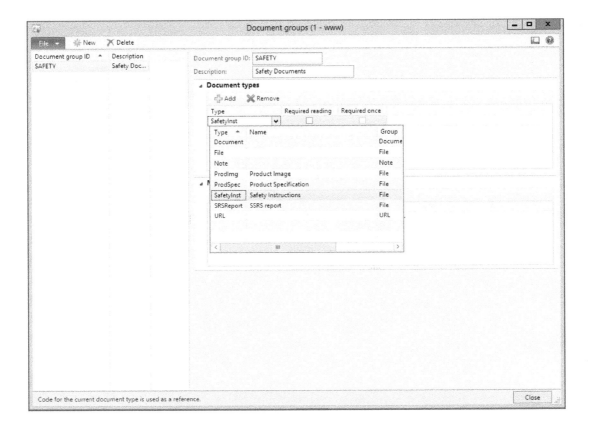

Then click on the **Add** button within the menu bar for the **Document Types** tab and select the Document **Type** that you want to use for the work instructions.

Creating Work Instruction Document Groups

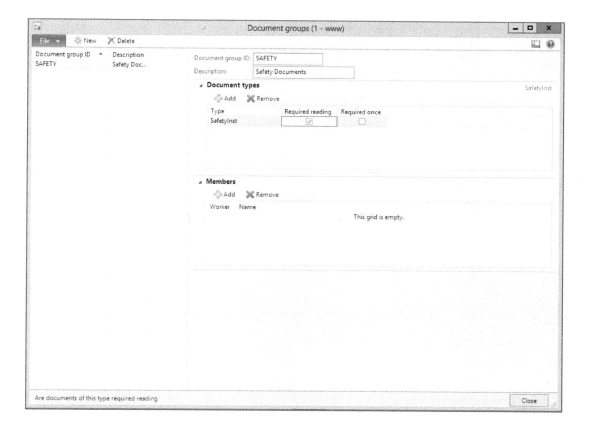

Also, if you require that the document is read before performing the operation, then click on the **Required Reading** flag for the Document **Type**.

If you want the worker just to read the document once as a refresher then you can also check the **Required Once** flag.

Creating Work Instruction Document Groups

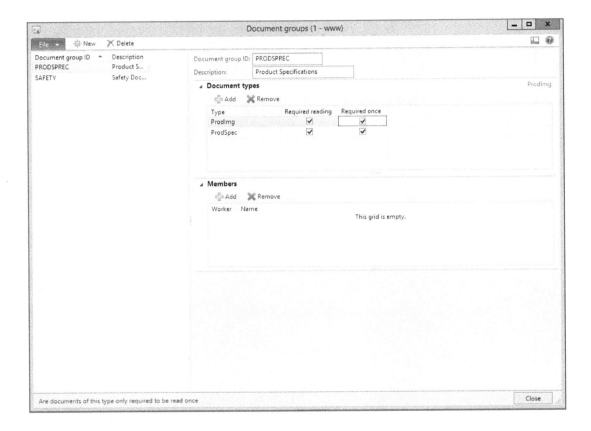

Keep on adding your documents until you have registered them all within the **Document Group**.

Creating Work Instruction Document Groups

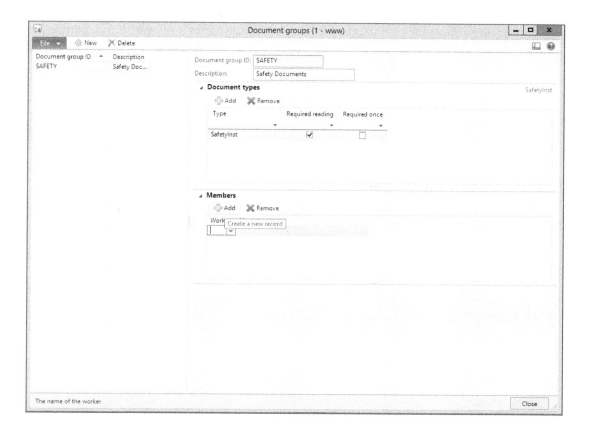

Also, if you want certain workers to have access to the work instructions, then click on the **Add** button within the menu bar of the **Members** tab to create a new record.

Creating Work Instruction Document Groups

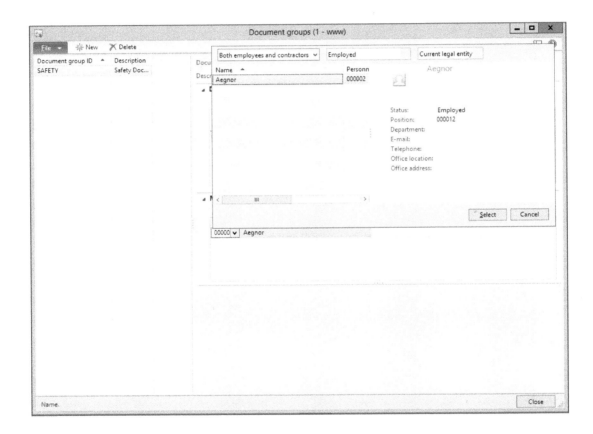

Then select the worker from the employee list and click the **Select** button.

Creating Work Instruction Document Groups

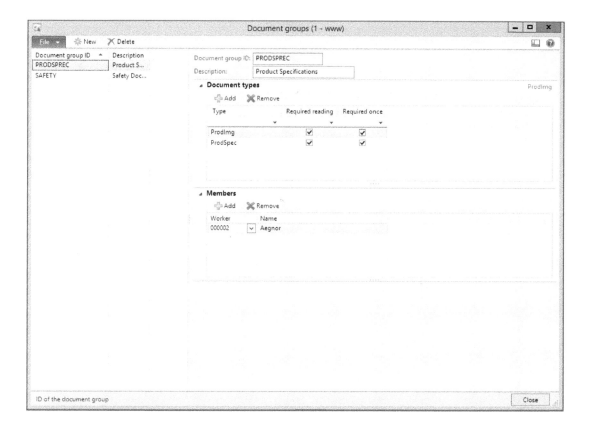

Keep on setting up addition **Document Groups** if you want to and when you are finished, just click on the **Close** button to exit from the form.

Attaching Work Instructions To Your BOMs

Now all we need to do is attach our work instructions to the appropriate BOM's so that production will be able to recognize them.

Attaching Work Instructions To Your BOMs

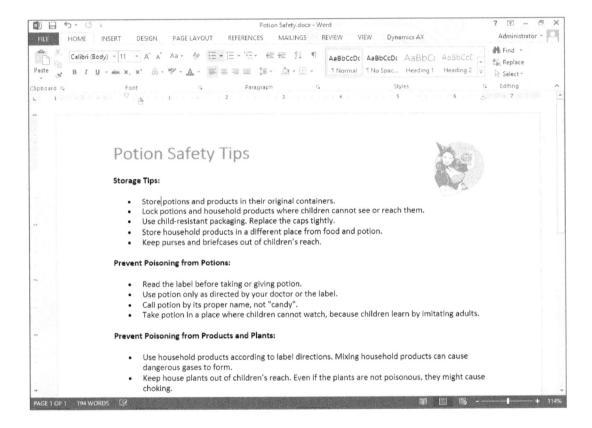

Start off by creating your work instructions.

Attaching Work Instructions To Your BOMs

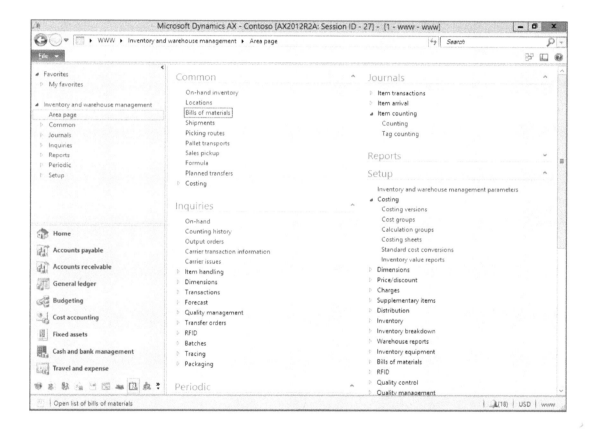

Then we need to open up out BOM's. We can do this through the **Released Products** maintenance form, or we can go directly to the **BOM's** by clicking on the **Bill Of Materials** menu item within the **Common** group of the **Inventory and Warehouse Management** area page.

Attaching Work Instructions To Your BOMs

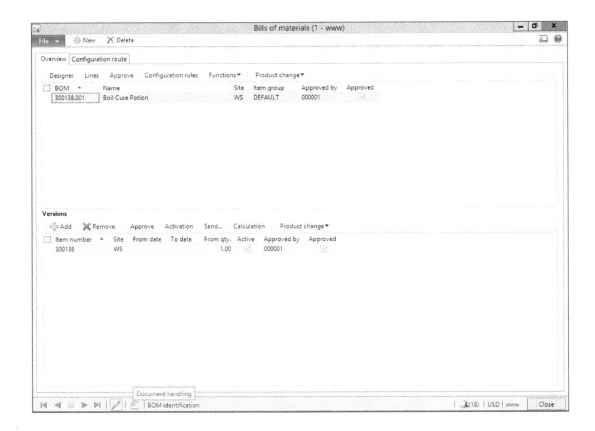

When the **Bill Of Materials** list page is displayed, select the **BOM** that you want to associate the work instructions with and click on the **Document Handling** icon. In this case, look for it in the status bar at the bottom of the form.

Attaching Work Instructions To Your BOMs

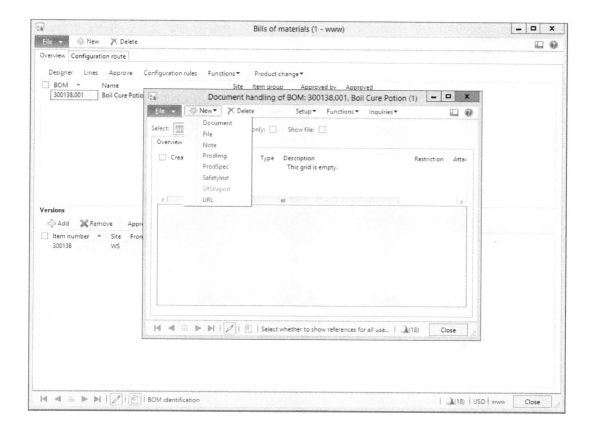

When the **Document Handling** maintenance form is displayed, click on the **New** button in the menu bar and select any of the **Document Types** that you have assigned to your Production **Document Groups**.

Attaching Work Instructions To Your BOMs

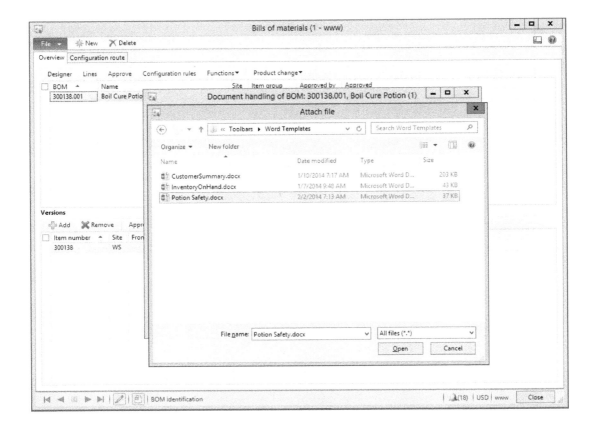

Then select your Work Instruction file and click the **Open** button to attach it to the BOM.

Attaching Work Instructions To Your BOMs

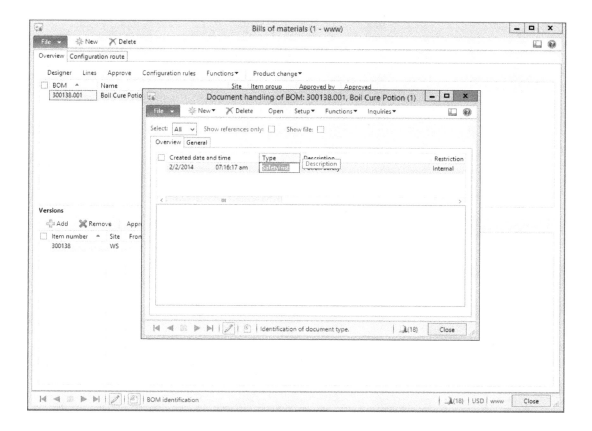

Keep on adding documents if you like, and when you are done, click on the **Close** button to exit from the form.

Viewing Work Instructions Through Job Registration

Now we can test out the work instructions through the **Registration Terminal.**

Viewing Work Instructions Through Job Registration

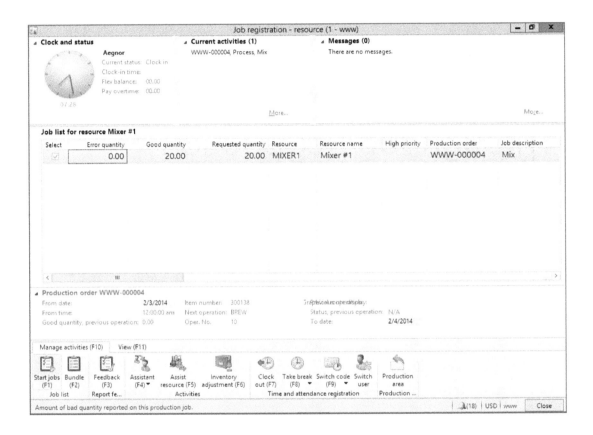

All we have to do to see this in action is to open up the **Job Registration** form and then click the **Start Jobs** button within the **Job List** group of the **Manage Activities** ribbon bar.

Viewing Work Instructions Through Job Registration

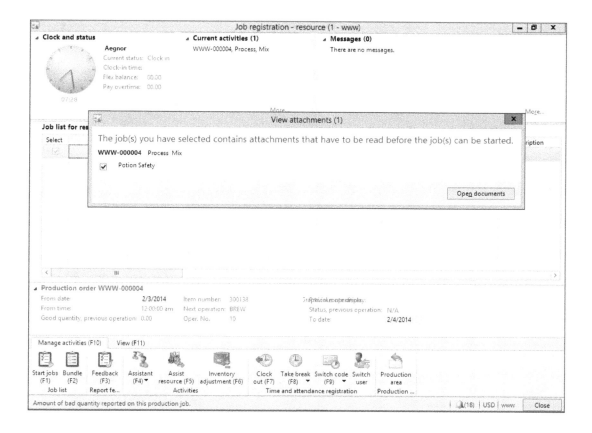

Before you continue on, you will be asked to read the documents that you associated with the BOM. To do this, lick on the **Open Documents** button.

Viewing Work Instructions Through Job Registration

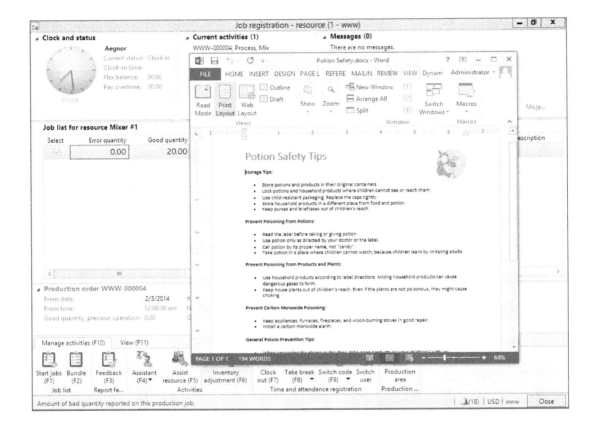

You will then see the document, and after studiously reading it, you can close the document.

Viewing Work Instructions Through Job Registration

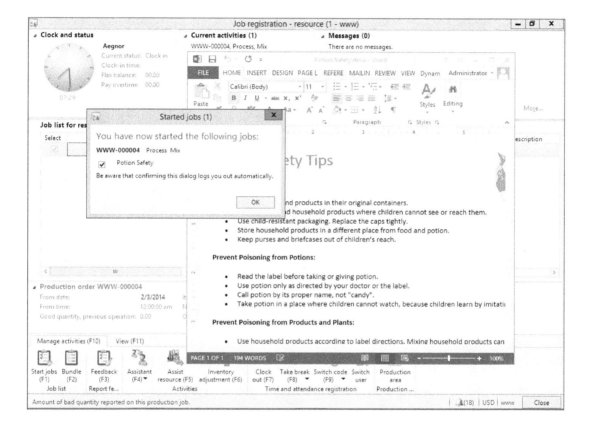

The dialog box will then allow you to confirm that you have ready the Work Instructions and you can click the **OK** button to continue on.

That was simple.

CONFIGURING COSTING SHEETS

One final tweak that you may want to make to the production area is to configure **Costing Sheet** formats. These are a great tool because they give you a better way to view all of your costing information. Not only do they allow you to group your costs into more logical groupings, but they also allow you to add additional surcharges and costs to your cost structure that is automatically included within the rolled up cost.

Configuring Cost Groups

The first step in the process if to configure your **Cost Groups**. These allow you to associate costs into common categories so that you can report off them more easily. Typical **Cost Groups** could be Packaging, Raw Materials etc.

Configuring Cost Groups

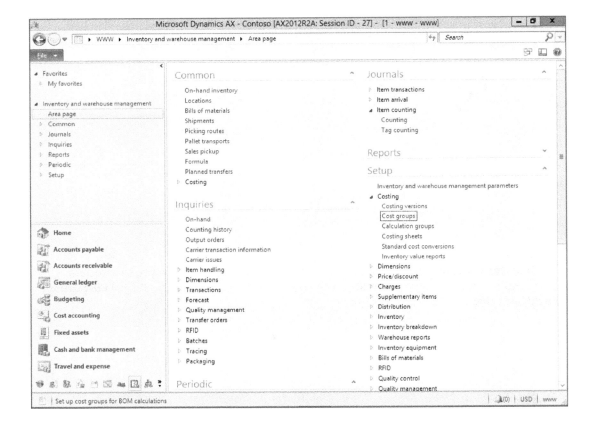

To do this, click on the **Cost Groups** menu item within the **Costing** folder of the **Setup** group within the **Inventory and Warehouse Management** area page.

Configuring Cost Groups

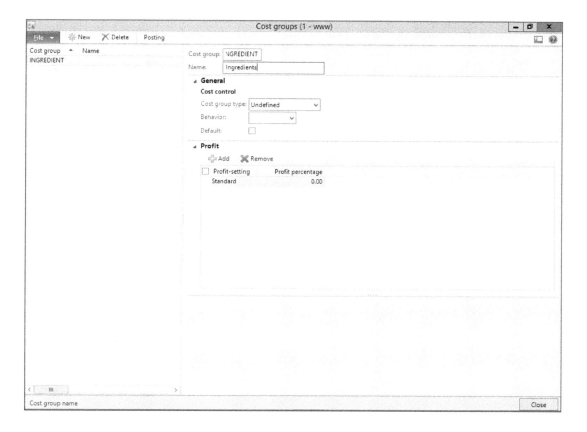

When the **Cost Group** maintenance form is displayed, click on the **New** button within the menu bar to create a new record and assign it a **Cost Group** code and a **Description**.

Configuring Cost Groups

Then within the **General** tab, change the **Cost Group Type** from **Undefined** to a more appropriate type. In this case we are assigning the **INGREDIENTS** to the **Direct Materials** type.

Configuring Cost Groups

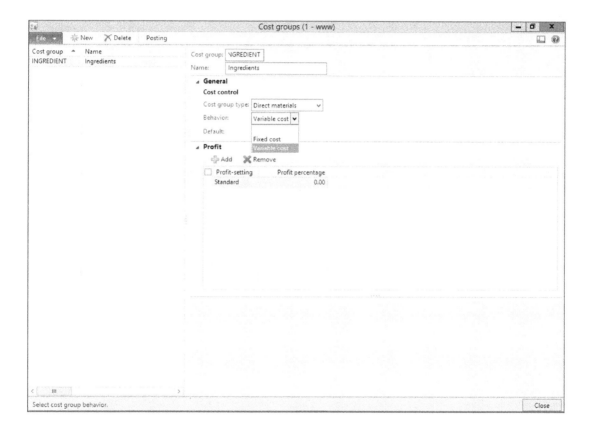

Also you can update the **Behavior** field to be either a **Fixed** or **Variable Cost**.

Configuring Cost Groups

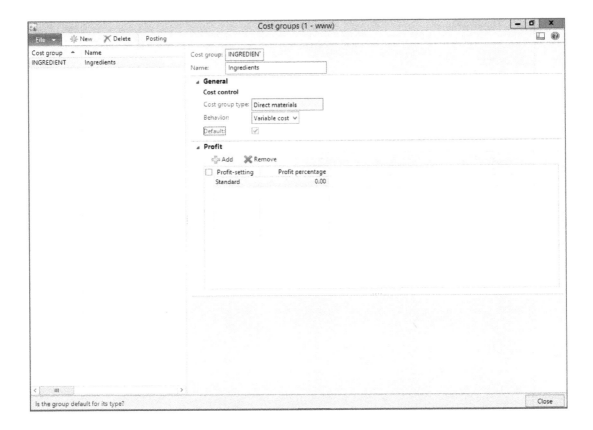

Note: At least one of the **Cost Groups** needs to have the **Default** flag set against it to mark it as a catchall cost group.

Configuring Cost Groups

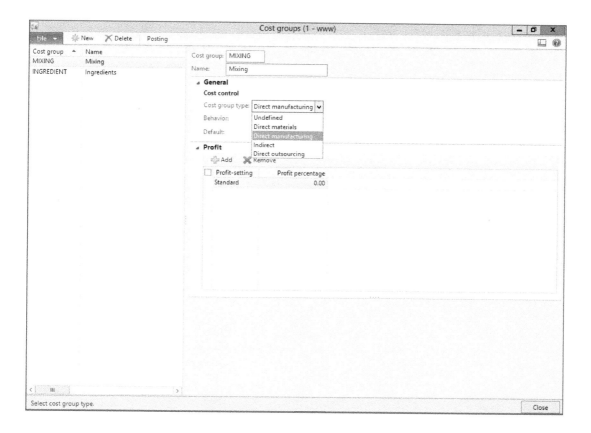

If you define any cost groups that are associated with the **Route** operations, then you set them up exactly the same way, but for those groups you will want to assign them a **Cost Group Type** of **Direct Manufacturing.**

Configuring Cost Groups

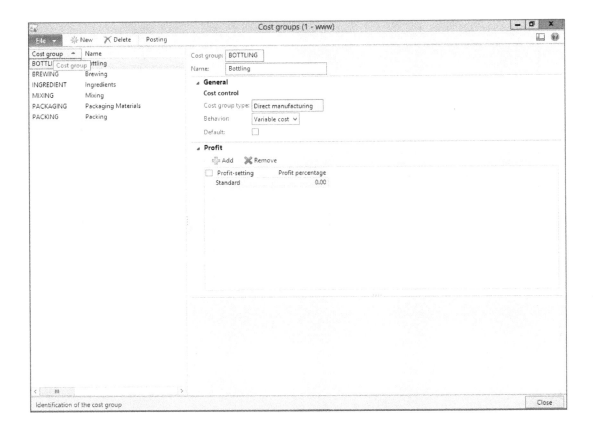

Repeat the process for all of the different buckets that you want to capture your costs within.

When you are done, click on the **Close** button to exit from the form.

Associating Products To Cost Groups

Now we need to return to our products and make sure that they are all associated with a **Cost Group** so that their costs will be allocated into the right cost bucket.

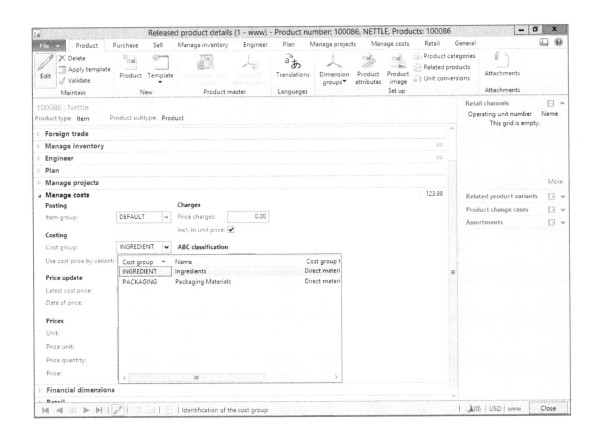

To do this, just open up your **Released Product** record and open up the **Manage Costs** tab. You will see the **Cost Group** field within the **Costing** group, and you can associate the product with the correct cost group.

Associating Cost Categories With Cost Groups

You also need to update your **Cost Categories** a bit as well. These need to have a **Category Group** assigned to them so that we can capture all of the manufacturing costs.

Associating Cost Categories With Cost Groups

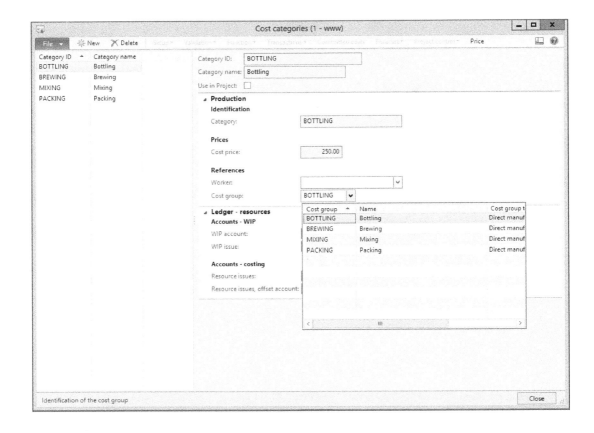

To do that, just open up your **Cost Categories** maintenance form, and for each of the **Cost Categories** assign a **Cost Group.**

Associating Cost Categories With Cost Groups

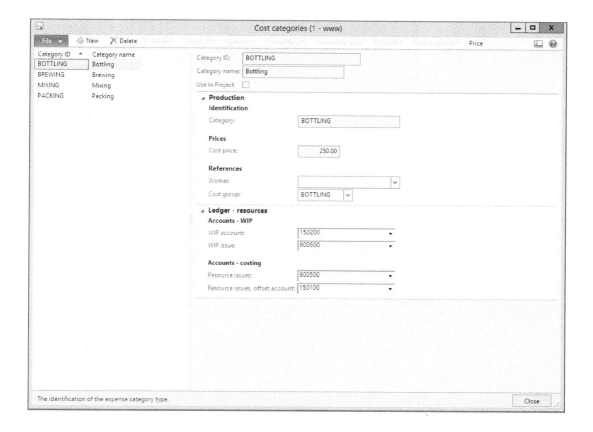

After you have updated all of your **Cost Categories** then click the **Close** button to exit the form.

Configuring Costing Sheets

Once you have all of the Cost Categories, and Costing Groups configured you can use them to create a Costing Sheet template. This will be used to gather all of your cost information and format it into a better format for cost analysis.

Configuring Costing Sheets

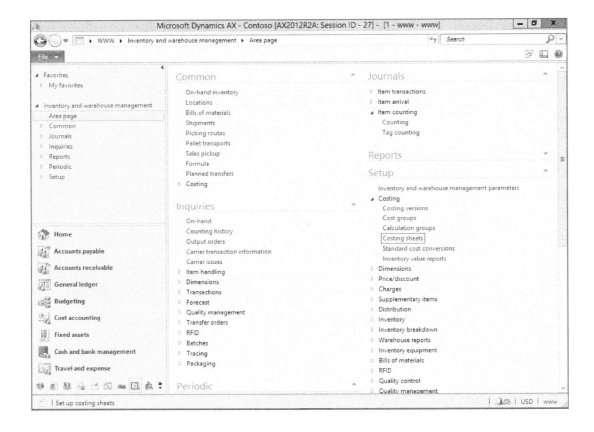

To do this, click on the **Costing Sheet** menu item within the **Costing** folder of the **Setup** group within the **Inventory and Warehouse Management** area page.

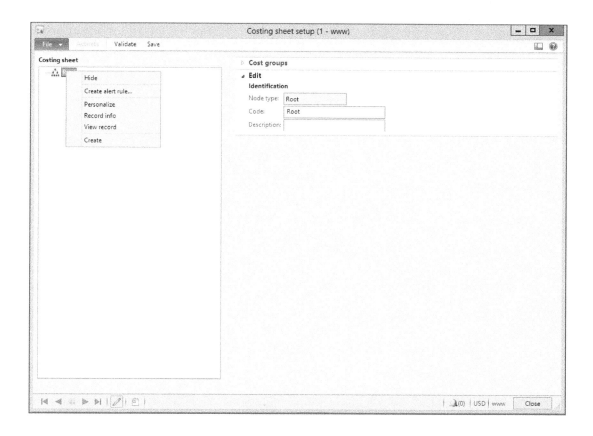

When the **Costing Sheet Setup** maintenance form is displayed right-mouse-click on the **Root** node and select the **Create** menu item to create your first level of the costing sheet.

Configuring Costing Sheets

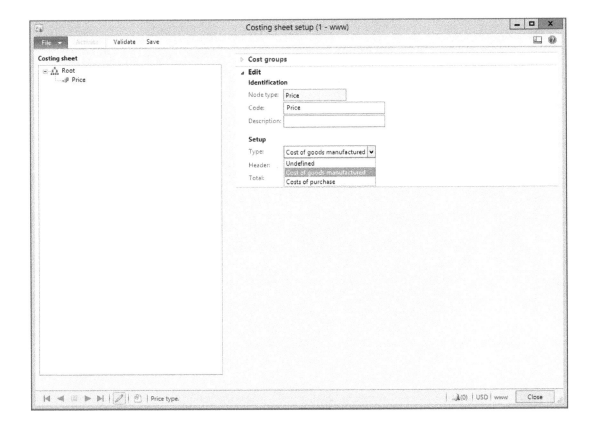

When the first node is created, click on the **Type** dropdown box and select the **Cost of Goods Manufactured** option to identify that this cost sheet is used to calculate the production costs.

Configuring Costing Sheets

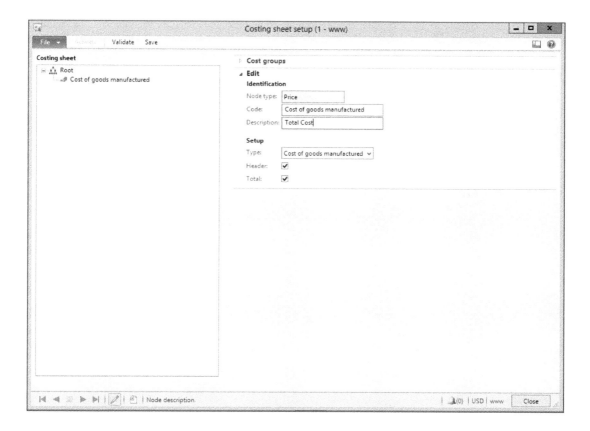

The **Code** will automatically populate and you can update the **Description** for the costing sheet node if you like.

Configuring Costing Sheets

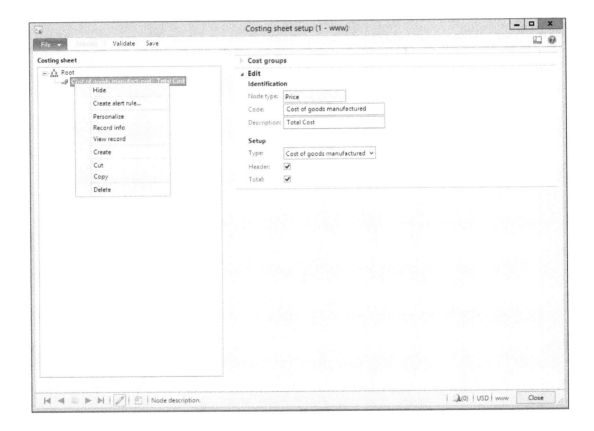

Now right-mouse-click on the new node and select the **Create** option again.

Configuring Costing Sheets

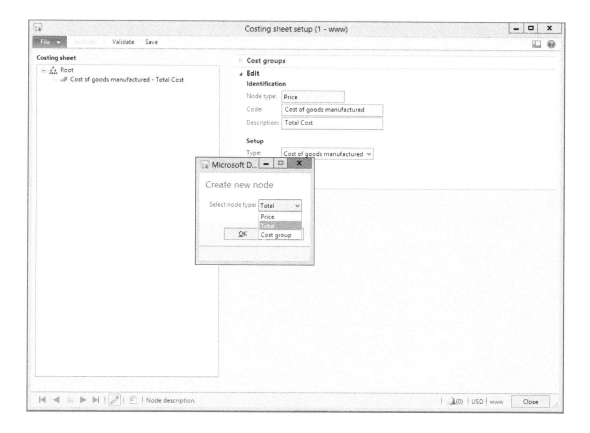

When the **Create New Node** dialog box is displayed, change the **Select Node Type** field to **Total** to create a total row that combines multiple cost group values together and then click on the **OK** button.

Configuring Costing Sheets

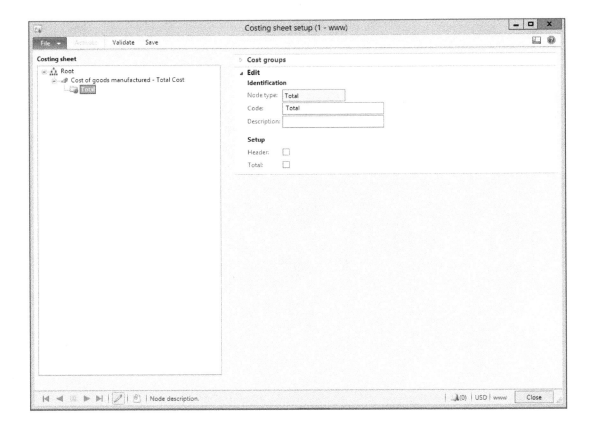

This will create a sub-node on the Costing Sheet.

Configuring Costing Sheets

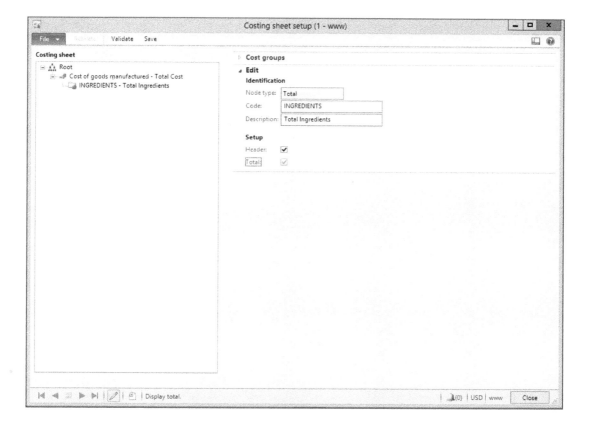

Change the **Code** and **Description** to be something a little more useful, and also check both the **Header** and **Total** flags.

Configuring Costing Sheets

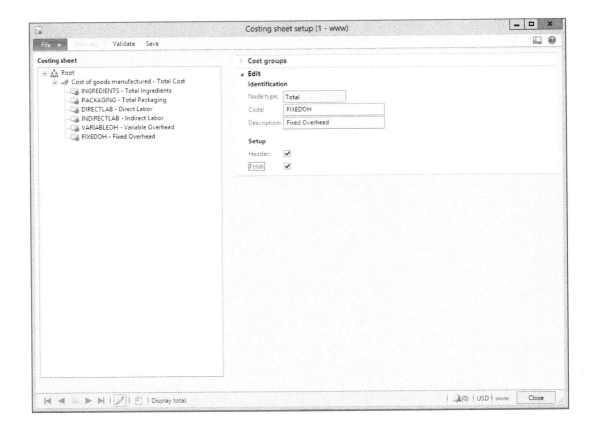

Repeat the process for all of the different groupings that you may want to use in your Costing analysis.

Configuring Costing Sheets

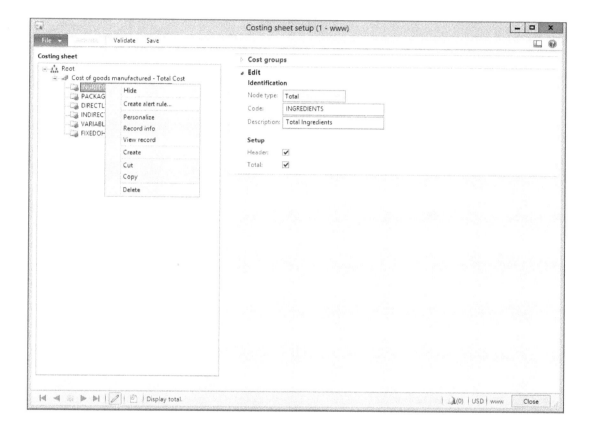

Now right-mouse-click on any of the heading nodes that you created that need to have Cost Groups associated with them and select the **Create** option.

Configuring Costing Sheets

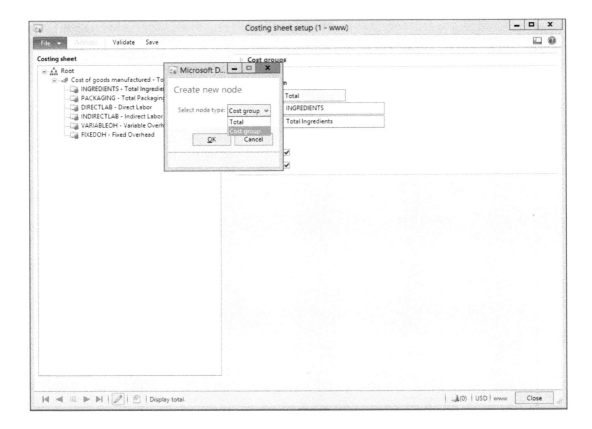

When the **Create New Node** dialog box is displayed, change the value of the **Select Node Type** field to **Cost Group**, and then click on the **OK** button.

Configuring Costing Sheets

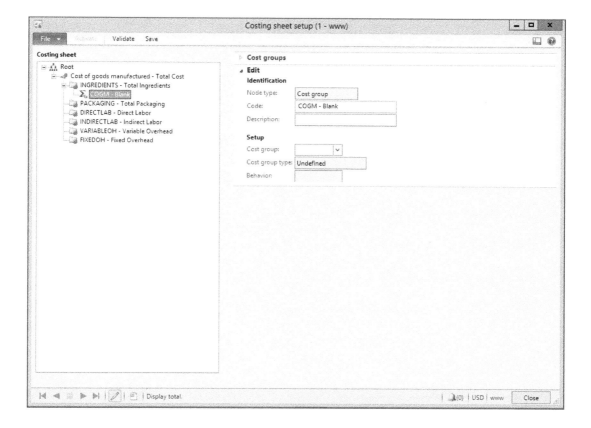

This will create a new **Cost Group** entry under the header.

Configuring Costing Sheets

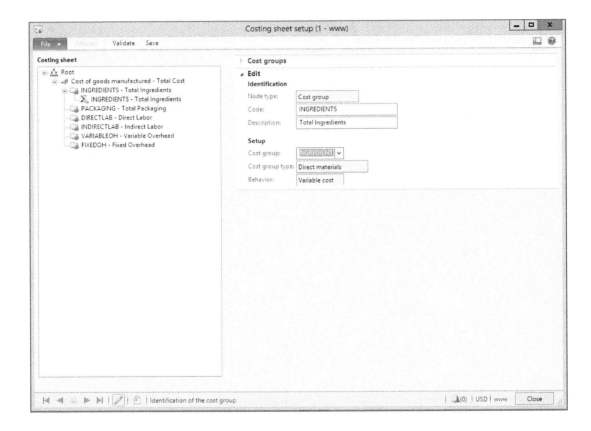

All you need to do is select the **Cost Group** that you want to include in the costing sheet level, and change the **Description**.

Configuring Costing Sheets

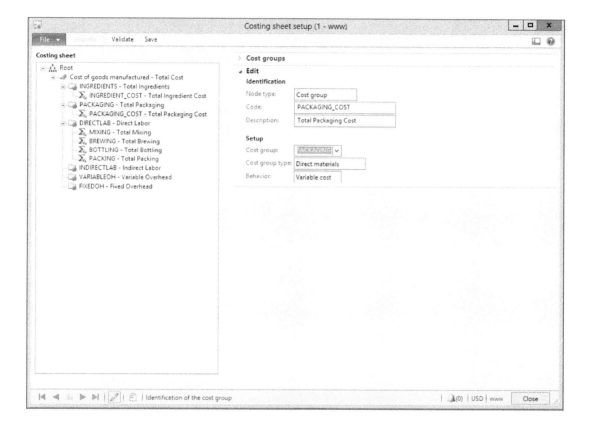

Repeat the process for any other **Cost Groups** that you have set up and allowcate them to different costing levels.

Configuring Costing Sheets

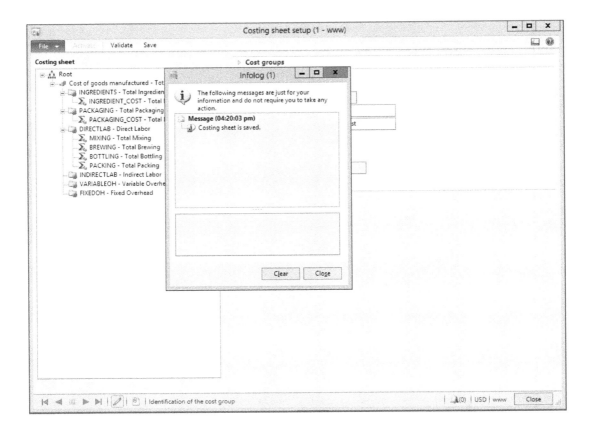

The final step in the process is to click on the **Save** button in the menu bar to save your costing sheet configuration.

After you have done that, just click the **Close** button to exit from the form.

Viewing The Cost Sheet Details

Once you have the **Costing Sheet** configured, then it will start popping up all over the place giving you a different way to analyze all of your costing components.

Viewing The Cost Sheet Details

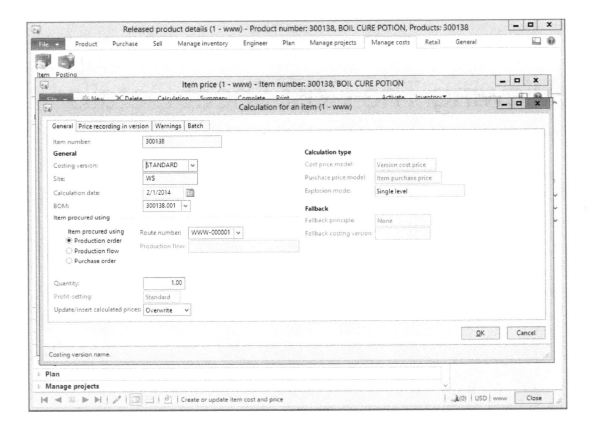

All you need to do is re-run your cost calculation for your item(s) to gather all of the costs again and associate them with the new **Cost Categories** that you defined.

Viewing The Cost Sheet Details

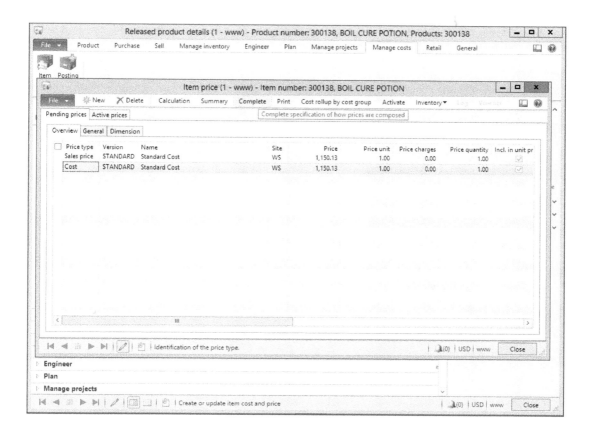

To see the new costing, open up your **Item Prices** and click on the **Complete** button in the menu bar.

Viewing The Cost Sheet Details

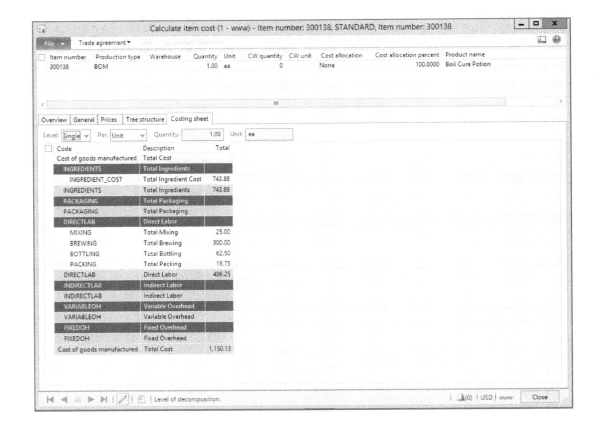

When the **Calculate Item Costs** form is displayed, if you switch to the **Costing Sheet** tab, then you will see all of your costs broken out and formatted in a neat costing sheet format.

That looks so much better.

SUMMARY

Now you have configured almost everything that you may need to model all of your production within Dynamics AX, but that doesn't mean that's all there is for you to take advantage of. Now that you are at this point, you may want to start investigating some of the other capabilities that are available within Dynamics AX.

Some additional capabilities that you may want to look at include the lean manufacturing capabilities, formula based BOM's for continuous process manufacturing, and extended costing capabilities through surcharges and fees.

About the Author

Murray Fife is a Microsoft Dynamics AX MVP, Author, and Solution Architect at I.B.I.S. Inc with over 18 years of experience in the software industry.

Like most people in this industry he has paid his dues as a developer, an implementation consultant, a trainer, and now spend most of his days working with companies solving their problems with the Microsoft suite of products, specializing in the Dynamics® AX solutions.

Founded in 1989, I.B.I.S., Inc. (www.ibisinc.com) provides distributors and manufacturers with next-generation supply chain solutions to maximize their profitability. A winning combination of industry and supply chain expertise, world-class supply chain software developed in partnership with distributors and manufacturers, and 25 years of successful Microsoft Dynamics implementations has culminated in making I.B.I.S., Inc. the preferred Microsoft Dynamics partner and solution provider for distributors and manufacturers worldwide.

EMAIL	murray@murrayfife.me
TWITTER	@murrayfife
SKYPE	murrayfife
AMAZON	http://www.amazon.com/author/murrayfife
BLOG	http://dynamicsaxtipoftheday.com
	http://extendingdynamicsax.com
	http://atinkerersnotebook.com
SLIDESHARE	http://slideshare.net/murrayfife
LINKEDIN	http://www.linkedin.com/in/murrayfife